# THE MYSTERIOUS DOOM

# THE MYSTERIOUS DOOM

## AND OTHER GHOSTLY TALES OF THE PACIFIC NORTHWEST

JESSICA AMANDA SALMONSON

ILLUSTRATIONS BY
JULES REMEDIOS FAYE

SASQUATCH BOOKS
SEATTLE

Printed in the United States of America

Cover design: Laura Pollack
Cover photograph and hand tinting: Jill Sabella
Interior illustrations: Jules Remedios Faye
Interior design: Lynne Faulk

Library of Congress Cataloging in Publication Data
Salmonson, Jessica Amanda.
        The mysterious doom and other ghostly tales of the Pacific
    Northwest/Jessica Amanda Salmonson; illustrations by Jules
    Remedios Faye.
            p.   cm.
        ISBN 0-912365-65-X : $11.95
        1. Ghosts—Northwest, Pacific. 2. Legends—Northwest, Pacific.
    3. Supernatural.  I. Title.
    GR109.5.S34 1992
    398.25'09795—cd20                                    92-25211
                                                            CIP

Published by Sasquatch Books
1931 Second Avenue
Seattle, Washington 98101
(206) 441-5555

TO W. H. PUGMIRE,
MY LOVECRAFTIAN CHUM

# CONTENTS

# Northwest Tales of Terror and the Supernatural

# THE MYSTERIOUS
# DOOM OF
# JOSHUA WINFIELD

J oshua Winfield was born a cold man with a cold heart, and lived apart from other New Englanders, despising everyone. The existence of humanity was such an imposition to Joshua that he hated merely to see a farmer off in the distance working in a field. So in 1874, Joshua sold his parcel of land, uprooted himself, and came to the Pacific Northwest, seeking isolation.

Could he have had a presentiment of the doom that awaited him, he might have stayed in New England. On the other hand, Joshua was such a strangely stubborn and unreasonable man, if he *had* had some precognition regarding his fate, he might have taken it as a challenge to a duel of wills, and come to the Northwest all the sooner.

He found a dark hollow in a wilderness that is today supplanted by Seattle's Mount Baker neighborhood. He selected a spot already partially cleared. Who had cleared it, and for what purpose, he did not yet know. But he was a lazy man, among his other faults, and the clearing allowed him to avoid a bit of labor.

The trees rose around the clearing, creating a verdant cage. Great cedars spread their limbs like enormous fans or blankets to keep out sunlight. Here, Joshua reasoned, he wouldn't have to see people passing along the dirt road; nor even observe so much as the smoke from the chimney of his nearest neighbor.

As luck would have it, Joshua had chosen to settle on the ancient burial ground of the Salish Indians. The Salish were justifiably distraught, but they were peaceable people whose complaints about white incursions were politely registered. A Salish man came around to warn Joshua of the spirits. A split-log floor had been laid, the whole-log walls were finished, and the shingled roof half done. Joshua stood before the freshly erected timbers, holding his rifle in the crook of his arm, glowering at the native who spoke quietly.

"There is not much sun reaches this place, and it is not a good place for the living to be. See up there?" The

Indian pointed to a sunlit rising, which was the only land visible above the trees surrounding Joshua's hollow. "That is a good place to plant a healthy garden. But in this place you have chosen, it is always cold, and the spirits will allow nothing to grow for you. It is dangerous to awaken the guardian of graves."

Joshua shifted his rifle from one arm to the other. There was nothing in him capable of respecting even the traditions of his own people, let alone the traditions of native people. So he chased the Salish man off, shouting rudely after him, "Here I've built my house, and here I'm determined to stay!" The native left, shaking his head sadly, and murmuring a Salish prayer. Joshua murmured, too, telling himself, "I'll not be scared off by foolish spirit tales."

Perhaps only the Indian's warning fueled the seed of superstition in Joshua. On a moonless night, in the soughing of the winds in the cedar branches, he thought he heard mournful chanting. It sounded as though it came from way up in the sky. Joshua ran outside his cabin, his rifle loaded, and searched all around, trying to locate the source of the chanting. He sought through the dark damp forest surrounding the hollow, telling himself, "That Indian is out here somewhere, trying to frighten me." But he could find no one in the vicinity.

On another night he awoke suddenly, certain he heard the soft padding of numerous moccasined feet outside, tramping down the accumulation of needles and forest debris. Once more he failed to capture anyone trying to give him a fright. All he spotted was a raccoon sitting in a tree, its eyes glowing with menace in the light of Joshua's upraised lantern.

Mists clung to his cabin like fungus to a rotting log. Even in fine weather, the hollow was damp and cold. A transient snowfall melted quickly from the surrounding forest, but clung to the ground where Joshua had settled. The sharp breezes whipped about the periphery of the hollow like so many impudent devils. Wind whistled through the chinks of his log walls, and down his chimney, threatening him in a tongue he could not understand. When his iron potbellied stove was filled with firewood, his cabin was still chilly. An inexplicably frigid spot hovered in a shadowy corner of his single-room dwelling, from which no amount of lantern light dispelled the darkness.

On yet another night he awoke with a start, lying in utter darkness, certain he'd been nudged by an insistent hand, hearing once again the whisperings in the rafters. That night he fled his cabin, running wildly through the forest until he came to the homestead of his closest neighbors, Thomas and Lucy Barton.

Since he'd hardly been on more than grunting terms with them previously, they were surprised to be roused in their bedclothes. Joshua was sweating from his long run, as well as from his fear. He was in such obvious distress that they welcomed him and heated him tea to settle his nerves.

He hated them for their friendliness. Or, rather, he so greatly hated to admit that he ever needed people that his disappointment in himself caused him to despise the Bartons. They put up with his grumpy, clamp-mouthed nature, and this annoyed him all the more, since by rights they ought to tell him he wasn't welcome.

For all his loathing, he depended on them more and more as the weeks passed, though he hardly more than sat and stared. He tried not to burst in at night again, but wandered away from his homestead in early evening, to escape his own fears in the warm presence of his neighbors. He remained incommunicative, but they tolerated him, and pitied him, for he was as nervous as a mouse and in obvious need of friendship he could not quite reach out for, even when it was offered. He was a stone of a man, self-sufficient in every way. That the Bartons dared pity him was just one more thing that angered his small soul.

As happened more and more, Joshua awoke drenched in his own sweat, his eyes gazing fearfully into the rafters. The branches of the surrounding cedars seemed to reach down and brush the cabin's roof, though no tree was near enough to do so. One day he climbed into the nearest trees and sawed off their lowest branches, until he was certain he had taken care of the source of his problem. Yet that night, he heard the light brushing of the roof's shingles as clearly as he had the night before.

The next evening, unable to face the weird sounds in his cabin, Joshua showed up unexpectedly at the Bartons. Lucy set to making cornbread, while Joshua and Thomas shared tobacco in long pipes. The tobacco settled Joshua's nerves, but for the longest while the two men spoke not a word. Then, for the first time, Joshua hinted of his nightly troubles.

"It's a bad piece of land I've taken," said Joshua. "But I cannot be defeated by it. I can't be run off by whispering souls."

Thomas puffed deeply, then said, "Joshua, you live too lonesome a life down there in the hollow. It makes the brain dwell on things too much. You ought to at least get yourself a dog."

Feeling criticized, Joshua decided then and there to master his fears in silence.

One day Joshua stood at the edge of his little failed vegetable garden, which had gotten insufficient light in the hollow. He gazed at the nearby sunlit hill, and for a moment considered dismantling his small house and rebuilding it up there. But his willful nature caused him to suppress such a reasonable notion; he could not bring himself to heed the warnings.

He tried to convince himself it was all in his own imagination, just as Thomas had suggested, or that the Indians were trying by various subtle means to scare him off the land. Then again, he thought, if there *were* spirits, he had no intention of being overcome by them. What was a spirit but smoke and air? Surely he could find a way to bring the situation under his control! By no means would he ever move his homestead elsewhere. Partly out of bravery, mostly out of pigheadedness and pride, Joshua stayed put.

Joshua's last night upon the earth was starlit and calm. The moon shone clear and bright. There was no wind. Neither did branches scratch his roof, nor were there any footfalls outside his wood-shuttered window. For a change, his little iron stove gave off a cheery warmth from its open door.

Joshua felt more peaceful than on any night since he had built his cabin. He nurtured the idea that the spirits, if there ever had been such things, had given up on him and moved to another place. Maybe they went up to that hill, he mused, grinning beneath his covers, thinking he had won the battle of wills.

Joshua drifted into slumber feeling safe and whole.

He had no idea what awakened him. He turned his head and looked at the open door of his wood stove, and saw two yellow coals glowering at him from inside. That was the only light. An otherwise abject darkness filled the room, and the silence was deathly.

He lay on his back and looked upward. He could not be certain he had seen a motion. He clutched at a frayed edge of his blanket, worrying it in his fist. For a moment he thought an owl must have gotten into his house. But if that was so, he should be able to hear it ruffling its feathers.

Still, he fancied something was descending slowly from the rafters, coming closer to his bed with every passing second. He told himself such things were not possible. Then he felt the impossible something light upon his cover so softly, it might still have been his imagination, or a harmless deer mouse. He kicked with his legs to knock the mouse away, if indeed anything was there.

In the next instant a weight bore down on him so heavily he could scarcely breathe. From head to foot the smothering presence held him. He tried to push it away, but it pressed even harder. He gave a bloodcurdling cry and managed to throw himself from his small bed onto the floor.

As it happened, the Bartons had been longer in town than they intended, and were coming home late by the light of the brilliant moon. Their horse moved slowly through the night, and all seemed peaceful and quiet until they heard the horrible cry. Lucy clutched at Thomas's arm and said, "Heavens! What was that?"

"We're near Joshua's homestead," said Thomas, stopping the buggy. He pried Lucy's fingers from his coat, then leapt to the ground and hurried down a narrow path into the hollow. He was certain Joshua had had a terrible accident, so awful was that cry; but now all was silent as Thomas threw open the door.

In a sliver of moonlight, Thomas could see Joshua Winfield spread upon his back on the floor, with eyes glazed white and his mouth twisted open in terror. Momentarily, Lucy stood at the door as well, and said, "Is he dead, Thomas?"

"Yes, he is, and he looks to have been scared to death!"

Thomas knelt beside the corpse, and could find no clue to an accident, no injury of any kind.

Lucy asked nervously, "What killed him, Thomas?"

"I don't know," Thomas replied. "And between you and me, Lucy, I hope we never have to find out."

In the years that followed, that cold-hearted settler was nearly forgotten. But among the Salish Indians, it was well known that a single white man lay beneath the soil of the sacred burial ground. When they chanted their songs to please and appease the spirits, the troubled soul of Joshua Winfield was included in their blessings.

# THE
# BARNACLE
# MAID

Out in Deception Pass, with the ebb and flow of the tide, the hair of a sea maiden can be seen drifting back and forth, back and forth, like a bed of kelp. Many people claim to see her even to this day. In her mortal life, this maiden had been the tribal princess Ko-Kwalawut, famed far and wide for her beauty and wisdom.

She lived before the coming of white settlers. In those days, the Samish people were famous fishermen. The coast-line was dense with ancient forests and the many streams and rivers were pure and clear. It was a paradise given to the Indians to oversee and defend, and during their steward-ship, the men were commonly out in their canoes, either upon the rivers or on Puget Sound. The women were more apt to be gatherers of clams, oysters, and crabs along the shoreline.

One day Princess Ko was filling her basket with shell-fish. She had struggled to dig up an especially large clam, but when she grasped it in her hand, it seemed to come to life and sprang into the shallows. She waded out to get the shellfish, but when she picked it up, it leapt into a deeper part of the water, as though upon invisible feet! She waded farther, and the same thing happened once more, so that she was standing waist deep in the cold, swift water.

When she started back toward the beach, a long nub-bly arm covered with sand and seaweed reached upward from the sand at her feet. It caught hold of her wrist and held her fast. She struggled to get free, but could not shake the chill and powerful grip. Then a voice from the water said to her, "Do not fear me. I, a prince of the sea, have greatly admired your beauty. I have fallen in love with you, and now that I have gotten hold of you, I will never let go."

"But you must let me go," said Princess Ko, a brave calmness in her voice. "Do you not know that I will drown if you drag me into your world?"

"How can I let you leave me after I have planned so

long to capture you?" the prince asked.

She moved her foot back and forth to see if she could uncover his face in the sandy sea bottom, but all she detected was the upraised arm. Still, when he spoke, she heard him clearly. He said, "If you will promise to visit me in this cove from time to time, I will let you go."

She agreed, and during each of their meetings, the sea spirit held her hand for longer and longer periods of time. He spoke loving words to her, and finally asked her to marry him. Princess Ko said, "Only the chief, my father, can give me into marriage. You must ask his permission, and I must abide by his decision."

The spirit rose out of the sea and followed the princess to the village. Princess Ko was unafraid, but the people were frightened of his appearance, for he was encrusted with barnacles. Seaweed hung all about him. He had eyes like a fish, perfectly round and with no eyelids.

Everyone dreaded the prospect of their beautiful princess marrying such a monster. His presence caused a coldness throughout the village. When he asked the chief for Princess Ko's hand, her father was incensed. He said, "No! If my daughter entered the sea, she would die!"

"She shall not die," said the sea's prince. "She shall become one among my people and live forever. I have such love for her, believe me, she would not be harmed."

"No! She is the pride of our people, and I will not permit her to go into the sea. Go away at once!"

An icy wind exuded from the sea spirit. His chest swelled, and he seemed to inhale all the luck of the tribe. His eyes narrowed with anger and his massive, encrusted fingers coiled into a fist. In a low, threatening voice he said, "If you refuse me, the water in all the streams will be undrinkable. The fish will depart. Your people will die of thirst and famine."

"Go! Go!" shouted the chief, angered by such threats.

So it was that the streams turned dark with foul scum and mud, or were made salty by the invasion of the sea, or dried up altogether. There were no fish to be caught, no clams or oysters or crabs to be found. Night and day, a coldness filled the longhouses, and bonfires burned without heat. The people grew thin and ill. The children cried out constantly for food and water.

Princess Ko went to the cove where she had often met with the spirit, and chastised him for his cruelty to her people. "How can I return your affection when you perform evil deeds?" she scolded. She demanded that he restrain himself from his heartless acts. If he would take away the curse, she would beg her father to permit the marriage. Hearing her words, the sea spirit relented a little, and there was almost enough to eat, although it was still a hard time for the Samish.

Princess Ko went every day to talk to her father, and at last he was convinced of her desire to marry the sea spirit.

He said he would give his blessing to the marriage under one condition. Once each year, his daughter must be allowed to return to the village, so that everyone could judge her happiness for themselves, and because otherwise they would miss her too much. The spirit arose from the sea until he stood atop the waters of Deception Pass. At the spirit's feet, water roiled furiously. The chief shivered at the coldness.

Then Princess Ko in her beautifully beaded and feathered wedding garments walked out on the surface of the water. She took her husband's hand, and slowly they sank downward together, until all that was visible was the beautiful dark hair of Princess Ko waving to and fro with the tide.

From that day on, the rivers ran crystal clear. Salmon hurried up the streams, coming from the sea, and the nets of the Samish people were filled. The beaches were dense with shellfish, and all the women's baskets were filled with razor clams and butter clams and oysters. There was greater prosperity than ever before, because the sea had married a Samish princess.

A year later, the princess came to visit. The salmon catch had been excellent the day before her arrival, which had been a sign of her coming, and everyone greeted her with reverence and awe. In spite of her friendliness, her relatives were uncomfortable around her, because Princess Ko exuded the terrible coldness of creatures of the sea, and this affected the atmosphere wherever she passed.

There was a great feast, and everyone danced and sang. Yet for all the joy of the reunion, a degree of superstitious dread underlay the festivities, for Ko's people felt strange about her new life. Her coloring had become ever so slightly mottled and greenish, and the chilliness her body generated made people want to sit or stand apart from her.

The following year there was another extraordinarily fine catch, followed by the arrival of the princess. But during the feast, everyone thought Princess Ko looked uncomfortable and agitated, as though she hated to be so long out of the sea. They feared her a little more than they had on her first visit, since strange things so often frighten people. Their fear made the princess melancholy in their presence.

The year after that, it was even more difficult for the people to get into a festive mood, despite so much food and singing. For by now, their beloved princess had undergone dramatic changes. Her beautiful eyes had become like the eyes of a fish, flat and round and unblinking. Upon her arms and on her neck, barnacles had taken hold. As she stood among her people, a cold wind whipped about her, and even her loving father could not stand close to her without shaking with a chill.

On the fourth year, she came again. The people were horrified. That face that had once been so beautiful was now entirely sheathed in barnacles. Her arms were like barnacle-encrusted driftwood. Seaweed clung to her everywhere. Only her raven hair was still the same, assuring the people that she was indeed their beloved princess.

Sad though it made her father the chief, he released his daughter from her vow to return once each year, for she was not happy out of the sea, and the people had become afraid of her coldness and appearance.

The Samish chanted this tale to the beat of drums. The old songs and the old ways are rarer now than they once were. But the people remember Princess Ko, and to this day her hair can be seen flowing to and fro with the tides. They say she is still protecting the Samish people.

# THE HAG'S
# HEAD OF
# ANGEL STREET

I t is common for children to experience hauntings. Some develop a dread of the darkness for this very reason. We are all familiar with the need of many children to have a light left on or to have the closet checked for monsters. Wherever do they get such ideas? Perhaps they know something adults have long forgotten—something with an element of truth to it.

Other children are not at all afraid of such things, although they believe in improbable stories as strongly as do those who fear the dark. The unfrightened ones take their invisible companions for *granted, as though all unknowns that haunt this world were friendly and protective. Parents think their children merely imaginative when they call these friends by the names they had in life, or repeat stories whispered to them from the other side.*

When little Wilum opened his eyes in the dark, it was to the sound of his sister whispering secrets to the shining thing above her bed. Wilum had no fear of what he saw, and his sister, rapt in conversation, was equally devoid of fright, although the apparition was thoroughly uncanny.

"Linda, who are you talking to?" asked Wilum, somewhat petulantly. He was only six years old. Linda was eight. These two children shared a bedroom in a white house on Angel Street in Seattle's Rainier Valley.

Linda lay on her bed at the opposite side of the room, gazing upward at a mysteriously shining face. "I'm talking to that head."

There were no nearby streetlights to bring such a glow to their curtained window, and no moonlight or starlight, due to clouds in the wintery night's sky. It was darker than dark, except near the ceiling, where a pale greenish light was shining from the one-dimensional image of an old woman's head.

"Whose head is that?" asked Wilum.

"It's not anybody's head," said Linda. "It's her own head."

Though flat as a piece of paper, the shimmering hag's

head was animated. Its mouth opened and closed, as though speaking to Linda, although Wilum couldn't hear it.

"Come over here, Head," Wilum called, feeling jealous of the way the head gave all its attention to his sister. It had a mass of wild hair and dark slits for eyes and mouth. Its face was lean and very elderly. If Wilum had seen it while he was all alone, he might have been scared. Since his sister wasn't frightened, neither was he. He didn't think it was fair that the head wouldn't talk to him. He wanted it to float above his bed instead of his sister's.

The fearlessness of children is often surprising. There are times when childhood innocence keeps such young ones as these from experiencing a justifiable nervousness. Wilum and Linda knew very little about ghosts, and accepted the presence of this one much as they accepted the existence of Santa Claus or Smokey the Bear. The world was filled with stranger things than floating heads, and they had not yet trained themselves to question the evidence of their own perceptions.

Had they known more about ghosts, they might have pondered how such things generally materialize in three dimensions, either transparent and resembling a hologram, or more substantial but shining in a blue aura, or most often as perfectly ordinary-seeming persons who quickly vanish when their presence is noticed. Even so, flat, one-dimensional ghosts such as the hag's head of Angel Street are reported now and again. It is possible that these entities are in some cases communicating from a dimension other than our own, so it shouldn't be surprising that they occasionally appear flattened.

The hag's head was intensely clear and vivid. Little Wilum's entire attention was focused on it. His skin had a funny feeling, a numbness such as happened when he slept on a hand, which seemed to be cold and dead when he woke up and tried to move it.

There was no sound accompanying the glowing image, insofar as Wilum could tell. The disconcerting thing was that Linda seemed to hear it and he could not. "Come to my side of the bedroom," he called to it in a whisper. "Tell me something, too." His jealousy that it had chosen his sister's bed over which to hover became acute. He whispered to Linda, "I'm telling Mommy you're talking to someone."

"You be quiet. I'm listening to the head."

"What's it saying?"

"She's telling me not to go under the bed."

"Why? What's under the bed?"

"She just says not to go under there. She says for me to go to sleep, but I told her I'm not sleepy anymore."

"I want her to talk to me! It's my turn! Tell her to come over here and talk to me."

"She said she can't go over there. Your bed is too far away."

"My bed is right here! It's close! Hey you, Head,

come here! Come talk to me!"

Linda said, "The head is saying your bed is *very* far away from her point of view."

The hag's head began to lower itself closer and closer to Linda. It drifted to one side and sank below the mattress's edge, then slid underneath the bed where it was no longer visible.

Wilum jumped up and ran into the hall. Linda jumped up, too, and went with him.

"Don't be a tattletale," said Linda.

"Then you tell her!" said Wilum.

They hurried down the stairs, their chorused, "Mommy! Mommy! There's a head in our room!" ringing out.

Their mother was watching a small black-and-white television in the living room, eating salty popcorn and drinking hot cocoa in the dark. There was no light in the room except for what came from the television, so that even Mommy looked like a ghost.

She looked at her hopping, chattering children. She seemed not to hear what they were saying, and certainly didn't believe them. She said, "The two of you march straight back up to bed and stop your roughhousing!"

"But Mommy! The head! Come and see the head!"

Mommy snapped, "If you don't get back in bed, I'll have your heads!" She set her popcorn bowl aside and pretended she was going to get out of her chair. She glowered with sufficient menace that the children squealed as they scurried upstairs and climbed into their beds.

They lay awake for quite a while without speaking. Wilum gazed toward his sister's bed, and saw that there was still a green glow underneath.

"Can you still hear her?" asked Wilum.

"No, the head is gone now. I can't hear her."

Wilum said, "I can see her glowing underneath your bed, though."

After thinking it over a long time, he climbed out of bed again, and got down on his hands and knees.

"What are you doing?" his sister asked.

"I want to see her," he said insistently.

Linda climbed out of bed, too, and got on her knees. They put their faces close to the floor to observe the green light. They could no longer see the head, even though there was still something shining with the same color. They both could now hear distant voices crying out, like animals or people screaming in the distance or calling upward from the bottom of a well.

"I'm going to climb under there and find out what it is," Wilum solemnly announced.

"The head said not to go under the bed," Linda reminded him.

"I don't care," said Wilum, still annoyed that the head had never spoken to him. "I'm going to get real close."

Linda said, "If you're going, so am I."

The two children crawled into the green light under the bed.

In the morning, their mother couldn't find them. No one ever saw them again.

# THE PHANTOM HOUND OF CHRISTMAS

B rutus, a Norwegian elkhound mix, sat in a cage at the animal control shelter, hoping for the best, entirely unable to comprehend how life had put him in this awful position. He was underweight and his stomach still hurt from the disgusting scavenged meals he'd found along the road before he was captured. His fur was mangy and dirty from the wretched places he'd had to sleep while on his own.

It probably hadn't been a very good idea to roll

around in the dirt and all over a squashed and smelly pheas-
ant, for after his capture no one gave him a bath. Somehow,
at the time, it had seemed a great and fun thing to do on
what otherwise had been a dispiriting day.

When the animal control officer had come in a big
green van to capture him with a loop at the end of a pole,
the man acted as if he thought Brutus might bite him. But
Brutus had never bitten anyone in his life. The officer
scared him half to death with that long pole, and that was
the only reason he had tried to escape. At the same time,
he was really hoping to be saved from his pitiful roadside
abandonment.

At the shelter he waited daily to be petted, to be fed
under a table rather than from a trough, to be taken for a
walk, to have a stick thrown for him, to have his matted fur
brushed. It would even be nice to be forced to have a bath
because he stank so much. None of these things happened.
His days were easier than scavenging along the roadside;
nevertheless, Brutus felt depressed.

For three days he had been sitting in this lonesome
cage waiting for something important to happen. He remained calm, and spent most of the time in one corner.
Vague hopes stayed always in his dog's mind, for, despite all
his troubles, he rather trusted people.

The ones who fed him daily and cleaned his narrow
space seemed like the sort he wouldn't mind getting to
know. But their friendliness was so distant and detached, he

could not make them respond to him. He was sure they were good and well-meaning, so why didn't they help relieve his distress? Couldn't they see he was eager to love them? Yet his wagging tail, his lolling tongue, his eager little woofs failed to move their hearts. There were cold barriers all around them, as though they were actually afraid to like a dog too much. Brutus had always prided himself on his ability to read the feelings of humans, but these humans were inscrutable. He felt an utter failure at being a dog.

The two-year-old Brutus never knew how close to doom he came. Dogs were brought in with such regularity, there was too little room to keep any of them longer than a week. Too soon the majority were "put to sleep," the euphemism for pet murder. This, unbeknownst to Brutus, was the reason the workers remained so aloof.

A healthy puppy or a small breed might last a bit longer, and had a far better chance of adoption. A fully grown and rather sickly elkhound was too big and homely to attract the glances of families with children who visited the shelter daily to take away one or another dog.

Then, from out of the blue, there appeared two friendly faces. Brutus instantly understood that he had found people to love: two men who were getting on in years, Ray and Leon. Brutus had seen them before, for he had been scavenging near their house.

They had called the animal shelter to begin with,

when they noticed an abandoned dog lurking along the highway margin. After a few days, they came by the shelter to see if Brutus had been claimed. They had decided they wanted the elkhound if his previous owners really had abandoned him.

The instant they appeared in that long corridor of sterile cages, Brutus knew his worrisome days were indeed over. His heart beat rapidly with expectation as the two men came toward him. They ignored the smaller dogs along the way and focused entirely on him. Their minds seemed to be calling out to him. Brutus stood and calmly moved toward the front of the cage, though underneath his calm exterior he was so excited he had to control the urge to pee! He stood by the door, ready to be let out, greeting the men who right from the start were like old and well-known friends.

Soon Brutus found himself welcomed into a home in the Kent Valley. He was lovingly nursed to good health, for he had been severely dehydrated and starving when first rescued. Brutus took an especial liking to Ray, and for the next thirteen years, Ray and Brutus did everything together. Brutus sat by Ray's chair when Ray was reading; he slept by Ray's bed when Ray was sleeping. They visited the city together; they went for walks in the woods together. Brutus was among the happiest of dogs. He and Ray were inseparable companions until, in January of 1984, Ray had a heart attack and was rushed to Swedish Hospital.

During Ray's hospitalization, Brutus mourned. He could not be consoled. He knew something was dreadfully wrong, so he refused to eat. He was now fifteen years of age, and that was quite old for a big dog. His health deteriorated rapidly without his best friend and, as much as he loved Leon, to be without Ray was incomprehensibly sorrowful to him. It was as though the world had disappeared.

The hospital refused to let Leon bring the dog to see that Ray was recovering well. But with the aid of the *Seattle Post-Intelligencer* "Action" columnist Maribeth Morris, a meeting was arranged, and the hearts of all Seattleites were soon moved by the bedside reunion.

It was not the first time the hospital had made an exception and let a dog visit a patient. But never before had the chief consideration been the dog's well-being rather than the patient's! A photo of a greatly relieved Brutus nuzzling his beloved master in the hospital bed was a page-one feature of the January twelfth issue of the paper.

Ray recovered, but clearly the elderly Brutus was on his last legs. They were quite literally his last legs, since severe arthritis made it almost impossible for him to use his hindquarters. His eyesight was failing as he approached sixteen. He was overweight—unable to exercise in his sedate old age and hopelessly addicted to chocolate bars and ice cream.

One day they took Brutus to the Pike Place Market, a place he'd always loved. Although he could no longer see where he was and had to be led slowly at the end of his leash, he nonetheless recognized the sounds and smells, and had a delightful outing. He became especially excited when he smelled ice cream. Ray said, "We really shouldn't feed him sweets."

Leon replied, "How can we deprive him in his last painful months?"

So a very happy old dog gobbled down an ice cream cone right then and there.

Ray and Leon nursed their old friend through that final year of life, until the vet counseled them that it really was time to put the suffering and invalid elkhound to sleep.

The two men grieved their loss. Brutus was often in their thoughts. They bought a personalized tile in the Pike Place Market with Brutus's name on it, a fine memorial. By chance, the tile was placed in front of a stairway to the lower level, the exact site where Brutus had eaten his last ice cream cone.

Throughout his life, Brutus had enjoyed Christmas, and in their grieving, Ray and Leon remembered Brutus on that holiday. It was their tradition to put a wreath in the window, and every year Brutus would sit for hours and admire the wreath, seeming for all the world to appreciate holiday loveliness.

During Christmas of 1985, the wreath was duly placed, but for the first time there was no Brutus to appreciate it.

He had been dead three months.

But when Christmas photos were developed, there in the picture of the wreath sat a spectral Brutus!

There was no doubt about it. Brutus gazed affectionately at his Christmas wreath!

After that, event piled upon event. A friend's visiting Great Dane veered from the place where Brutus used to sit, and afterward backed out of the way and appeared to be watching an invisible presence strolling across the room and out the front door.

During an attempted car break-in one night, Leon, who was hard of hearing, woke to Brutus's barking. For this reason alone, the thief was foiled.

Ray experienced the ghost dog bumping into the side of the bed each night, just as he had done in life. At first Ray thought the sensation was spooky, but afterward he said, "It's great to know Brutus is still here."

News columnist Jean Godden tried to find rationales for these events. The placement of the market tile—a pleasing coincidence. The Great Dane recognizing Brutus in his favorite spot—a lingering odor of the animal. We may add a little wishful thinking on the part of the dog's loving owners, who missed him greatly. But the columnist also saw the Christmas photo, which was harder to explain. She admitted, "It does have a ghostly image," and concluded the evidence was worth considering—that Brutus had come back.

# THE
# HEADLESS
# COLONEL

O h, Penelope! Hoo–hoo!"
I turned slowly on the crowded downtown sidewalk
and saw an enormously fat gentleman waddling in my direction as fast as he could, which wasn't very fast. He was
waggling all ten of his stubby fingers at me, and wheezing
and panting, he called again from the short distance re-
maining between us.

"Penelope! Are you still interested in haunts and
ghoulies?"

It took me a moment to place who he was. Ah, yes! James something-or-other. I'd met him twice at meetings of a fraudulent occult society that, on my second visit, I was forced to expose to the public due to its predatory manner of charging the elderly, lonely, or grieving to receive purported messages from their departed loved ones.

I was not in the habit of shouting my interests on street corners, but it is my philosophy never to be embarrassed. At James's cry of "haunts and ghoulies," several passersby gazed at the fat gentleman, then at me, my frumpy, commonplace appearance doubtless seeming quite a contrast to the man who was hailing me and for what purpose. James pulled up alongside me like a ship to a pier's piling as I replied, "How have you been, James? Still attending those old-fashioned Age of Aquarius séances?"

"Why, no! Not since that day you leapt on top of the table and cut the silk thread that upheld the trumpet. What a thrill that was! Much better than the horn's silly tooting! But I do keep looking for something, well, you know, 'weird' in this world. And I think I've found it! Want to stay in a haunted house with me?"

Now it was true James didn't seem like a masher who'd make so foolish a pitch in order to get a rather conservative lady into a house with him for the night. On the other hand, I had only met him twice, and he was a decidedly odd fellow, though nice. I wasn't sure how to reply.

"Unchaperoned?" I asked, and was glad he caught the

edge of humor in my voice.

"Why, Penelope, you surprise me! We'll have a chaperon, all right. The ghost! I'm a bit leery of it myself and want an expert along. What luck to have run into you here! You *are* still doing your supernatural research, aren't you?"

"Certainly. We all have our idiosyncrasies. I'm sure it will be my lifelong avocation. Where is this house you speak of?"

"It's the Ebey farmhouse on Whidbey Island."

"Ah! The Headless Colonel," I remarked. "He's well known. I've often thought of investigating the site. But isn't it on park land? I wouldn't think they'd let anyone stay there at night."

"There's been some minor vandalism—kids, you see. They enter the park when it's closed, looking for the ghost, and end up throwing rocks through the windows of the farmhouse. As a member of the Historical Preservation Society, I volunteered to sleep in the place during summer weekends, when kids have been the most troublesome. No one else wanted to do it. Some were leery of the ghost, others just thought it was too rustic and bothersome, as there's no electricity. But I thought it was a perfect opportunity to find 'the weird' I've always looked for. Unfortunately, on the two weekends I've been there so far, I was too scared to wander away from my Coleman lantern. I guess I'm a bit of a coward about these things, though I try not to be. I've been looking for someone to bold it with me, and you're such a brave sort, Penelope."

I chuckled at the very idea of it taking bravery. "It takes a little knowledge, that's all. Then things just aren't quite so frightful," I said.

James and I were walking along side by side. I noticed that other pedestrians were having trouble getting around us, for James took up more than an average amount of sidewalk and was rather slow. I led him across the street and we ended up in Shorey's, a quaint used bookshop. James trundled down a staircase and piloted himself sideways between narrow rows of books.

"This is my second-favorite bookstore," said James. "The Book Center in Belltown is number one." He scanned a few titles as we wandered about, and finally we docked—oil tanker and tug—alongside a little-perused section of the store, where Bibles were congregated. Being in nobody's way, we stood conversing.

"The original house," said James, "was burned to the ground in 1860, three years after the murder of Colonel Ebey, but shortly afterward it was rebuilt. The Colonel never seemed to know the difference. I'll be heading back to the island in my old pickup truck late this afternoon. Will you come?"

"It's awfully short notice," I said. "But I've nothing planned for the weekend, so…"

"Great! It'll be an adventure!"

That afternoon James's smoking rattletrap of a pickup truck stopped outside my residence. It had begun to rain, and there was a good wind up—hardly weather for an outing—yet sitting on the flatbed was a large picnic basket James had prepared. I eagerly tossed a sleeping bag and night case in the back of a truck, covering them with a tarp to keep the rain off, then climbed into the cab seat alongside James.

We were off to the Mukilteo ferry and were soon after bouncing along the island roads toward Coupeville. It was only sprinkling a little, so James kept turning his windshield wiper on and off. The wiper on my side didn't work, and the one on his was badly worn. All along the drive, James and I exchanged some of what we knew of the ghost of the colonel who died so gruesomely.

"Reports of his walking spirit go all the way back to territorial days," said James. "The kids around here refer to 'the evil bluff' in hushed tones, and commonly dare each other to visit it by night. Many of those kids have seen the Colonel, but not many people take kids seriously. When I talked to a couple of them, they didn't sound like they're trying to fool anyone. They're convinced."

"I'm sure they have every reason to be convinced," I said.

South of Coupeville, James pulled his old truck into the absurdly named Sunnyside Cemetery. The sloping graveyard had a grand view of Ebey's Plain. We got out of the truck, each with an umbrella, and stood gazing toward the plain, the rundown farmhouse clearly visible. At the edge of the plain was Perego's Bluff, and a beach beyond that.

"Here's where the headless chap is buried," said James, pointing out an age-worn tombstone that read, "Colonel Isaac A. Ebey, January 21, 1818–August 13, 1857."

I found the graveyard too prosaic. I'd visited really wonderful graveyards in New England, from a time when eerie "death's heads" were popular—winged skulls with the most alarming scowls and grins. And my English journeys were even more remarkable for graveyard visits. For us here in the Northwest, an 1850s gravestone seems so old, but an old English kirkyard has amazingly antiquarian dates, and, what is missing in America, graveyard poetry!

"When I'm dead and buried," I said, "I do hope I can have a better stone than this. I'd like a poem on my stone."

James said, "Oh yes, something like, 'Here I lie in mucky rotten sodden flesh and all forgotten.'"

"James! That's dreadful. Wherever did you hear it?"

"Dunno. Graveyard potty, I suppose."

I grinned at his vulgarity, then said, "I wrote an epitaph once, inspired by my English graveyard tour:

Are we recalling fleeting joys?
Or our pitiful errors?

Are we dreamers resting sweetly?
Or caught in nighted terrors?
Pity us, dust and bone
Beneath the grass, alone.

"Penelope," James commented, "I had no idea you were so morbid."

"Why else is one fascinated by the dead?" I inquired.

"Well, for me, I suppose, it's just that I'd like to know things don't end."

"Ah yes," I agreed. "If there are ghosts, then there must be an afterlife. Even a wretched survival is better than none at all."

James said, "I'd hoped you'd keep me in good cheer on this adventure, Penelope. But you're a bundle of dark thoughts. I wouldn't like to live eternally as a headless ghost like the Colonel. But don't you think there must be a heaven that such poor creatures have just somehow failed to locate?"

"I do like to think so, yes," I confessed.

James lumbered beside me along the bluff. The wind had risen so that we couldn't use our umbrellas without them turning inside out. Though the rain was slight, it was slowly soaking us to the bone.

James, his picnic basket on one arm, said, "I'd hoped for better weather. I guess we'll have to picnic in the farm-house."

The view was splendid, the waters of Puget Sound sweeping away from the bluffs. I said, "Look there, it's dry under those firs."

"So it is," he said happily, and aimed his huge body in the direction of the trees. Soon we were sitting upon fir needles. James had made rather a lot of sandwiches — tuna, cheese, bologna, and jelly. "What's your favorite?" asked James.

"Oh, tuna, I guess."

"I make a great tuna salad sandwich," he said boastfully, handing me an example of his gourmet's art. And I had to admit it was pretty good.

"Candy bar?" he offered, there being several in the bottom of the basket.

"Not for me, thanks."

James was silent for a while, stuffing his face with several sandwiches. I couldn't help but think he wasn't doing his heart any good. At length he asked, "Do you like life, Penelope?"

His question took me quite by surprise. "What sort of question is that?"

"Well, you're kind of a specialist in death."

"In ghosts, at any rate. I rather think I get more enjoyment out of life than most people."

"I envy you, then. I'm so scared of dying, but life isn't much either. Sometimes I think the only things I can enjoy are eating and sleeping."

"And you call *me* morbid!"

"If I could overcome my fear of ghosts," he said, "maybe I'd overcome my fear of dying."

With an attitude of self-loathing, James threw a half-eaten sandwich—his fourth or fifth—into the basket and said, "And maybe I wouldn't have to eat so much."

"If it works," I said, trying to bring up his spirits, "you and I can write a diet book, *See Ghosts and Lose Pounds.*"

James sighed through his big puffy lips, gazing into the overcast distance. He said, "The Colonel sometimes walks along this very path. But not before dusk. Have you ever known of a daytime ghost?"

"Yes, many."

"Truly?"

"Certainly. Most people are more sensitive to them in the quiet of the night. But ghosts aren't restricted to the darkness."

James gazed along the bluff expectantly, his mood somewhat improved. He said, "But I've only heard him after sundown, and he was killed at night."

"That does make a difference," I allowed.

The passing moodiness of James notwithstanding, it was a lovely outing, despite the rain. If nothing more came of it than a graveyard visit and a picnic on a windy bluff, I should be satisfied.

James showed me around the farmhouse. He had prepared a single loft room for himself. He had a Coleman stove and lantern on a card table, and a cot in the corner. The furnishings were very minimal. "Do you mind the sleeping arrangements?" he asked. "We can put on our nightshirts in another room, but I hope you're not concerned about our sleeping in the same room. It's kind of, well, scary, and I'd like not to feel alone this time."

"We'll be just like kids on a camp-out," I suggested.

"Great! You can have the cot and I'll sleep on the floor with all my bedding, snug as a bunny."

"You said you've heard the ghost nights?" I asked.

"Oh yes. You'll hear him too, opening doors and the like. I've never worked up the nerve to leave the room, but with you along, I'm sure we'll get a glimpse of him. From the hallway you can see down the stairs to the front door. That's where he was killed. Do you know the story?"

"I've not managed to get around to doing much research on Colonel Ebey. It was a revenge raid by Haida Indians from the Queen Charlottes, wasn't it?"

"The Haida weren't usually a violent people," said James. "But one of their medicine men had been brutally murdered by whites. So they set out to find a white medicine man to get even. They'd come down the coast specifically in search of one Dr. John Campbell, but he wasn't home. Instead, they found Isaac Ebey, against whom they had a grudge anyway. He had once shot an Indian woman for stealing potatoes from his garden."

I don't know what time it was when I awoke. It was extremely dark. I had heard the floorboards creaking, for James was moving about. I heard him working with matches and the white-gas lantern.

"What's going on?" I asked wearily.

"Did you hear it?"

"All I hear is the hissing of that lantern."

In the next moment, the intense white light of the lantern's mantle erupted, and James in his nightshirt was limned in platinum.

I heard a creaking door opening somewhere in the house.

"Hear that?"

"Sure."

I climbed out of my sleeping bag and put on a wrapper.

James said, "I—I—I think it's show time."

We crept into the hallway. Overcome with protective manliness, James led the way, despite his fears, carrying the hissing lantern. He walked on naked tiptoes. Every step of his bulk made the floor creak.

We gazed down the stairs from the loft. James turned off his lantern, for the whole main floor was ashine with a blue light. We saw a figure moving about, carrying a musket.

"It's Isaac," James whispered, and the floor under his feet began to vibrate because he was shaking so much.

"Don't have a heart attack on me," I said. "Calm down a bit."

"But it's the ghost."

"It would seem."

The spirit was a dark, man-shaped shadow in the blue light. As he moved toward the door—slowly, as in a dream—it opened, and he went out. From our vantage point, we could not see outside. I prodded James to make him go nearer. He went halfway down the stairs before he froze to the spot. In a constricted voice, he said, "The Haida are out there."

Out in the night, an envelope of light illuminated only itself. Nothing was visible in that light, but outside its circle were silhouettes of Indians dressed for battle, armed with long knives. One of them wore a mask. The silhouette of his head sported a long, birdlike beak.

Isaac Ebey stood with his back to the farmhouse, holding his musket. We could not hear him, though he seemed to be speaking. The Haida were in no mood to listen. They fanned out around him, less fearful of the musket than he may have expected. He aimed at one of them, but as the musket fired—we heard it like a distant explosion in a tunnel—a hatchet struck the weapon and caused Isaac to miss his target.

In the next instant, the Haida were upon him. They held him, stretching him by his arms. The man with the bird mask raised a long knife. With one swipe, Colonel

Ebey was beheaded. As his head fell to the ground, the light went out, and the Haida and the Colonel were gone.

Since James had doused his lantern, we were once again in darkness. He whirled around on the staircase and began to run straight at me in the dark, shouting, "Wo-oh-oh-oh!"

I had not previously seen him move quickly and had doubted he was capable of it. But now I could barely keep ahead of him. The scariest thing about the night was that I was nearly squashed and trampled.

He ran into the loft room and buried himself in his bedding, shaking like a rabbit. I was tempted to suggest to him that his diet wasn't working, but it seemed not to be the moment for levity. Instead, I tried to soothe his nerves. "They're gone, James. There's nothing whatever to worry about." But he was whimpering, and I doubted he was listening to me.

I went down the staircase to the front door. It was closed and latched as we had left it earlier in the evening. I unlatched it and stepped outside. The sky was still overcast and misty, but some diffuse moonlight made the landscape barely visible. Near Perego's Bluff stood Colonel Ebey, holding his head in his hand.

The severed head's eyes were glowing. The mouth was wide open. From that gaping maw issued forth the wail of a banshee.

Then Colonel Ebey drifted away over the bluff and

vanished in the misty night over Puget Sound.

I heard James coming up behind me. He put a hand on my shoulder, saying, "Are you all right?"

"Certainly. Are you?"

"I made a fool of myself."

"God made all of us to be fools."

"God, you think?"

"Or a Goddess. You're not scared now?"

"Me? Of ghosts?" asked James. "Pshaw. All the same, if the ferries ran this late, I'd be glad to load into the truck and get the hell out of here."

We spent the rest of the night without event, and the next day James took me home to Seattle. I didn't see him again for nearly a year. When by chance I ran into him, I hardly recognized him. He'd lost sixty or seventy pounds. Maybe that ghost diet book wasn't such a bad idea!

# THE POOL
# OF THE
# MAPLE GOD

The city of Victoria was called Camoosun by the first settlers, who were ruled by the Hudson Bay Company in days when company ships anchored alongside Chinook Indian canoes by the white sands of Cadboro Bay. When Sir James Douglas first founded Camoosun, the tribal peoples found him curious and appealing. They greeted him warmly, doubtlessly to their everlasting regret. All too soon the whites dwelled in a wide fort enclosure with armed guards sitting in watchtowers at intervals around the settlement. Pioneers in many such places inevitably seemed to express a singular inability to get along for any length of time with natives.

Fort Street was in those early days so swampy that it was more goose pasture than road. Blanchard Street went to the gate of the fort and ended, as though the wilderness beyond the gate were too alien and distant for more than an overgrown footpath. There were no other streets to speak of, only trails linking one pioneer home to the next.

The surrounding forest of oak, spruce, maple, and fir was like an ancient cathedral where gargantuan deities appeared in the form of striding mist, receiving sustenance from slants of sunbeams and worship from bears and nesting eagles. The crowns of mighty oaks, a thousand years old if a day, rose so high as to mingle with the clouds.

Sir James, exploring the forest as something of a naturalist, chanced upon an extraordinary tree at the end of a tortuously winding trail on a steep hillside. It was a sturdy maple, a species destined to become the symbol of the nation. Split into several enormous trunks, it stood above the earth on a network of fat roots. Amidst these roots sprang forth a crystal spring that was the sweetest water Sir James had ever tasted, and he instantly shared the same awe of the place that Indians had already experienced for generations.

The spring seemed to bleed upward from the roots, and, even in the hottest summer, there was a startling coolness about the water, as though it had flowed from a glacier.

The Chinook claimed these waters had medicinal properties, and settlers found it difficult to disagree. That maple was called by the name of a God, and a nymph was said to dwell in the spring, to whom the God was married. If a woman looked into the waters during a full moon, some believed she would see the man she was destined to marry. If a man looked into the water, he saw the woman he was one day to wed. People also believed that barren women could drink of the spring and become fertile. The Chinook held that if the God-tree were ever chopped down, then the nymph would leave, and with her would go the miraculous well.

In 1860, D. W. Higgins, whose future successes were to include his role as speaker of the British Columbia legislature, was a young adventurous man who heard the local legends and forged his way on horseback to the place of the mystic well. With him were several companions, young men and women from Victoria. Higgins drank of the waters and discovered that, true to the legend, they were icy cold though the day was hot. The young people who had followed him got on their knees before the pool and strove to see the faces of their future wives or husbands. But one of the girls remarked, "It won't work unless the moon is shining in our faces, and here it is midday."

The outing was so pleasant that the site became a favorite picnic site and spa. Every Saturday, Higgins organized excursions on Indian ponies for young men and women. They brought bathing suits and swam in the cold, cold waters, splashing gaily, laughter rising amidst the maple's leaves like tinkling bells.

The well became known as Undine, after the water nymph of Lafontaine's romantic poem and la Motte Fouqué's novella. The tree they named Father Time. Thus, the old Indian legend had been Europeanized, and all the young people expected marital benefits to arise from these coed outings to the place of Undine and Father Time.

It wasn't until two years later, in August of 1862, that Higgins sought "to test the pretty legend," as he called it. On a night of the full moon, he saddled his horse and set out for the well. He hardly expected to find anyone else there, but unknown to him, young couples commonly went there to test their futures. As he descended the winding path, he heard the voices of two men and two women. "Ho!" cried one of the young men. "Who comes here at such an hour?"

Higgins said, "I've come to see the face of my future wife."

Laughter rang up the hillside. "Come down, then," called the same young man. "We're all here to take a peep."

The other young fellow said to one of the girls, "You look first, Darlene."

"I shan't," Darlene replied. "Suppose I see the most loathsome fellow's face, all covered with warts and wens?"

THE POOL OF THE MAPLE GOD

"'Tis my face you'll see," said her beau. "Have I warts and wens?"

The other young man, who was only slightly older than the others, dashed to the spring's edge, saying, "Well, if you're all afraid to look, I at any rate must find out." He got on his knees and, with the moon full in his face, looked down. Everyone waited, hardly breathing, such was their expectation. He stood, brushed himself off, and momentarily replied to their unspoken queries. "I saw my own reflection plain enough, but that's all."

"It would be like you to marry yourself," said the younger man.

Higgins tried his luck with the same result of seeing only his own face. He stuck out his tongue, and so did his reflection; he squinted his eyes, and so did his watery image. "What a humbug! There's nothing to those old legends after all."

One of the two young women strode forth quite boldly, knelt by the pool, and gazed earnestly at her own reflection in the moonlight. The men were babbling meanwhile about the foolishness of Indian legends, posturing importantly because Darlene stood amidst them and they hoped to impress her by their lack of belief. Each pretended never for a moment to have fallen for such silly superstition. Then, unexpectedly, Darlene gave a short cry and pointed toward the well, saying excitedly, "Oh no! Look at Annie!"

Annie lay face down in the icy waters. Higgins leapt

to her in an instant and pulled her from the spring, laying her upon the grass beneath Father Time. Each of her four companions took a foot or hand and rubbed life and warmth back into her. After a few moments she came to her senses but fell at once into a hysterical fit. "Take me home!" she cried. "Take me home at once!" There was fear on her visage, yet she gave forth peals of unearthly laughter.

On their ponies and heading for town, the two women chatted, the one trying to calm the other. When things seemed quite settled down, the other girl asked, "Annie, what on earth happened to you? Why did you carry on like that? You frightened us all."

"I saw the face," she said.

"Oh my! Was it your future husband?"

Annie shivered. "It was the most horrible face I've ever seen. Horrible! I felt as though it wanted to devour me. And the most awful eyes! He reached his hand out of the water to catch me by the throat, and that's when I fainted. I'm not even certain it was human. I could never marry anything so evil. I'd sooner die!"

The ride to town was too far, so they stopped at a farmhouse. By then Annie was so weak she could no longer ride. A chill surrounded the whole group, so they warmed themselves by the farmer's hearth, then borrowed his horse and buggy to arrive in town very late in the evening. The story spread like fire, and the popularity of that frigid spa dwindled considerably. Higgins no longer organized outings, having not the heart for it.

Annie Booth fell into a melancholia from which she never fully rallied. She had always been rather a strange girl, or so people said, but for this sudden turn downward, the mystic pool was often blamed.

In April of 1868, Benjamin Evans, a retired usher of the Supreme Court, was working in his garden overlooking Cadboro Bay when he saw Annie, dressed as if for a Sunday service, start along a winding path toward the long-shunned Undine and Father Time. It had been a long time since anyone had seen her looking so well, and Benjamin hoped she had overcome her trouble. He called after her, "Annie! What are you up to?" But she ignored him, and vanished along the way. He shrugged and went back to his gardening.

Later that evening, an Indian lad happened along. He saw Annie sitting quietly at the side of the pool. She held her face in her hands and was weeping. She rocked to and fro, moaning miserably. The Indian felt himself to be intruding on some secret anguish, and so slipped away without her noticing he had been there.

In the dark of the night, the Indian lad awoke at his campsite, and called, "Father! She's crying out! She's crying for help!"

The boy's father was instantly alert to the alarm in his

son's voice. "Who's crying for help?" he asked.

"A young Englishwoman I saw at the Pool of the Maple God."

His father sat up in his covers and listened intently to the sounds of the surrounding forest. "You young fool," he said. "That's a cougar calling to its mate."

Sighing with relief, the boy lay down and went back to sleep. But in the morning, he was astir early, and went to the spring. He could not see the Englishwoman of Victoria, but saw her hoop skirt, her turban, her scarf, her corset, and other garments scattered about the ground and hanging upon bushes. He pressed nearer the springs, and gasped at what he saw. He ran back to the campsite and told his father.

Benjamin Evans joined them along the way, and came to the pool where Annie Booth was floating face up, and weirdly beautiful, like Hamlet's Ophelia. There were no marks upon her, but amidst her strewn garments she had left a note, which read, "Today I realized who my husband was to be! I have rushed to his embrace, for only he can ease the misery that is in me."

The old Indian—the lad's father—insisted that no ill luck was ever associated with that mystic pool. But, he said, the pool was incapable of untruth. That poor girl had seen Death reflected in the pool because it had been her fate, for Death was her one and only destined partner.

But the whites in Victoria had taken a very great dread

of the place. To the distress of the Indians, who considered the area sacred, a vandal seized upon Father Time with axe in hand and flung the tree to the bottom of the long slope. The pool Undine vanished that very day, and the site where once tree and pool had been slowly eroded and at last fell into the bay.

# THE
# LAST
# PASSENGER

When I was a young man, I had an overblown sense of my own dignity and importance. I could never have revealed my horrible adventure to anyone, for fear of being called touched. Now I am old, and the elderly are allowed to be eccentric. I feel free to tell what happened.

The surrounding hillsides were denuded of trees. A region that once was a shady forest had long ago become a landscape of dry grass with an occasional, incidental fir. At the foot of one hill stood a glorious old mansion with a peaked roof, balconies, a large front porch wrapped around two sides, and a yard hemmed in by ornate wrought-iron fencing. Nearby was a stable long in disuse, a smaller barn still in good repair, a crumbling water tower, and a few splendid maple trees between the tower and the house.

My grandparents owned Azalea Farm amidst the grassy knolls of Douglas County, Oregon. My father's people were easterners, and I was fresh from an eastern university. I had come west to make my mark. My maternal grandparents' house was my first planned stop, a resting place where I could spend the summer months sorting my options.

I had passed on the chance of being a junior partner in a large, well-known law firm in the east, for I had no desire to be one of many, a youngster amidst the staid, where my opinions would rarely carry weight. Rather, I believed the west to be still a place where youth was not a demerit, where I could swiftly place myself as an influential man.

I intended to practice law either in Oregon or Washington, but was not yet certain of the specifics. There were school chums in Portland, and that seemed my most likely destination. My only certainty (or so I thought) was that wherever I chose, I should instantly become a lion of society. But for the time being, I needed only to relax in newfound freedoms and take in the country air.

Late one morning, I was sitting on the porch smoking a pipe. It was a hot day, an hour shy of noon, and cicadas were whirring. Suddenly I sat forward, for I saw a six-horse stagecoach coming down the road.

I had not heard about any local festivals, and I had never seen such a contraption stored anywhere in the vicinity, so the sight took me quite by surprise. I leapt up and ran in the house, calling to my grandfather. He was involved with a book from his private library. He looked up with what I thought was a profoundly disinterested gaze. I couldn't induce him to come and see the coach. He said, "It's gone by now, John."

That didn't seem at all likely to me. Annoyed by my grandfather's lack of enthusiasm, I went back to the porch to watch the stagecoach alone. But my grandfather had been right. The coach and its six horses were gone.

Despite the heat of the August day, I was suddenly chilled all over.

In those days, there were few who questioned the existence of ghosts. Not even a young man with an eastern education was apt to be a doubter. Ghosts were taken for granted by most people, unlike in our modern age wherein scientific theories alone are accepted on faith, until the next theories supplant them.

After I saw the stagecoach, I began to ponder the many small disturbances I had encountered in my first weeks at Azalea Farm. Things had occasionally moved from where I'd put them. A comb once leapt from an end table before my very eyes, without visible cause. I approached my grandfather about these phenomena, but he said only, "This is an old house. Of course it's haunted." Beyond that, he could be induced to say nothing.

My grandmother was less tight-lipped. Though she would not speak of spirits, she loved to tell the history of the house.

Azalea Farm never grew azaleas. Rather, its name came from its location across Cow Creek, just off Azalea Road. It had originally been a stagecoach stop called Galesville. In 1882, Grandma's ancestor Dan Levens built a livery sufficient for ninety horses. A territorial colonel, Zedekiah Stone, operated six-horse stagecoaches through the Sexton and Siskiyou mountains. Every morning at eleven, the northbound stage stopped at Galesville.

The stage line was established long before Levens built his stable and turned his house into a hotel. Previously there had been a stockade on the land, an outpost on the main road between Jacksonville and Roseburg. In 1855, Captain Rinearson, along with thirty-five enlistees from around Cow Creek, put down an Indian uprising. Among those enlistees, and among the Indians as well, were some of my own ancestors! My mother's family had lived in Douglas County since the 1850s. When you add in the fact that my grandfather was one-quarter Indian, then we'd had family members here from time immemorial.

"The present farmhouse," said Grandmother, "was rebuilt in 1931 from the remains of the old Galesville Hotel that burned earlier that year. So only the barn and livery and a few parts of this rambling building are Victorian. If you go out back and take a good look at the big shade maples, you'll see some of them still show fire scars. They were planted by Dan Levens in the 1880s, and survived the fire."

In a few weeks, I had "used up" all the romance I could squeeze out of my family's history and the sights of Douglas County. It was too rural for me. I was beginning to think more and more of Portland or Vancouver. The summer heat of Galesville was stifling, and the cooler weather of Portland beckoned. Mostly I was bored out of my mind.

Although my overblown dignity made me feel too important to patronize local taverns, one day I felt there was nothing else to occupy me. I drove about thirty miles to a roadside bar and accidentally drank myself unconscious.

The next day I awoke in a back room that the bar owner kept for the purpose. He was extremely kind, but I was so embarrassed to have discovered I couldn't hold much liquor, I fear I was a bit rude to him. I hurried out to my grandparents' Ford and sped away. The bad taste in my mouth was as much from my behavior toward the barkeeper as from my ridiculous binge.

I got within four miles of Azalea Farm when the tire

blew. I was not as alert as I should have been, and drove off the shoulder into a ditch. Cursing, I got out of the car and started walking. My head still buzzed, my mouth was dry, and I realized I was sufficiently dehydrated that the hot sun just might cause me to pass out.

Then I heard the rattling of the northbound stage. I stood to one side of the road and turned to see it coming. The six horses in their harnesses were gorgeous animals. The driver gazed straight ahead. He had a look on his face that struck me as stupid and bewildered. I thought to myself, "He *knows* he's dead!"

In the broad light of a summer day, who can fear a ghost? I certainly did not. The driver pulled the reins and the horses halted. He looked down from his high seat and said to me in a monotone, "Need a hitch to Galesville, son?"

What possessed me, I'll never know. But I had been so intensely fretful about my need for water, I really couldn't adjust my thinking.

"Thanks!" I exclaimed, and approached the side of the stage. The door opened slowly of its own accord, and inside I saw a woman in a Victorian dress and two men with silk hats in their laps. I climbed into the coach and greeted them with a smile, but no one spoke. The young woman held a feathered fan and seemed to be suffering from the heat. As the stage began to move, I noticed that the outside world was greatly muffled. I could not even hear the sound of the horses.

I quite understood I was riding with ghosts. I don't believe there was anything of drunkenness still lingering about me. Nevertheless, I was in a very odd frame of mind, and wanted to make the most of this extraordinary meeting.

"Where are you traveling from?" I asked boldly. The two men with hats in their laps turned their cold gazes on me. Only then did I feel a chill. I turned to the woman on my left and said, "It's a dreary hot day for a trip, isn't it?"

She lowered the fan from her face. I saw beneath her bonnet not flesh, but bone. I gave a little yelp, then noticed the two men's faces had also turned into skulls.

My careless attitude was instantly broken. I shouted, and threw open the coach door. I almost leapt out, except that I could not see the ground. There was only mist—such as one might expect in San Francisco or Seattle, but certainly not during a Galesville summer.

I hung at the edge of the doorway gazing outward into nothingness, not knowing what to do. I turned and looked at my three companions. They were decayed and extremely horrible. One of the men raised his bony hand as though to assist me. I so dreaded his touch that I gave another loud cry and leapt into the mist.

It seemed as though I were falling for a very long time, on the verge of losing consciousness, a wet wind swirling upward and around me. I say "seemed" because I was by then in a high state of panic and barely able to think or feel. After long minutes, I saw what at first I thought was my grandfather's face appear from out of the mist. Only it was not my grandfather at all. It was an elderly Indian who resembled him. He grabbed my out-flung arm and yanked so hard I thought he was going to pull it out of the socket.

When I opened my eyes, I was lying at the side of the dusty road at Azalea Farm. My grandmother and grandfather were hurrying toward me from the house. I didn't know what to say to them. My grandmother asked a flurry of questions, but my grandfather said, "Leave the boy be, Myrtle. He'll tell us what he wants to when he wants to."

But all I told them, when I was able, was that I'd had a flat tire and driven into a ditch. I never told anyone what actually happened—until now. Despite my secrecy about the event, I was a greatly changed man because of it. I was far less full of myself in the years that followed. So, scoff at my story if you will. But there are things beyond human knowing—evil things and good things. A little more awe, together with a little less certainty, might improve all of us.

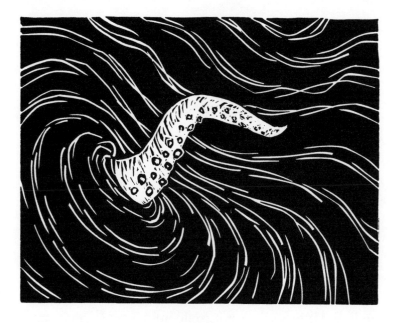

# THE
# FABULOUS
# SEA BELOW

It was from old Samuel Keplemann that I first learned of the fabulous sea below. The hermit of our rural community on Vancouver Island had come from no one ever knew where, and kept to himself in a warped, leaning, unpainted, termite-infested shanty. The stovepipe was bent and rusty, protruding from a tar-papered roof. Grimy flour sacks hung as curtains behind cracked panes.

They weren't the best circumstances in which we met. I was a high school rowdy then, big for my age and a bully. I had broken into his shack to rob him.

Once every three or four months, old man Keplemann ventured down from the blue-spruced hillside to load
up on provisions. He always paid with solid gold pieces.
The coins were engraved with peculiar characters and
profiles of half-human heads. These valuable objects were
a topic of interest whenever Keplemann came to town.
The popular theory was that the old codger had uncovered
a pirate's chest. Never mind that the theory was outlandish!
The only pirates ever to harbor in the north of Vancouver
Island dealt in bad whiskey, not the doubloons of earlier
epics and other seas. Yet it could not be denied that curio
shops would happily provide booklets and photos regarding the renegade sea captains who once lurked off our
coast, awaiting the clippers out of Puget Sound. Popular
"knowledge" of that sort did seem to give credence to the
pirate-chest theory, although the most casual reading of
those souvenir booklets would reveal the theory's ridicu-
lousness.

Ridiculous or not, the strange coins were real. So one
day after school, I took my motor bike along trails leading
to that laughable shelter. Seeing neither smoke from the tin
chimney nor kerosene lamplight in the window, I decided
to break in and find out if there might be a cache of ancient
gold coins hidden on the premises.

My dirt bike left leaning against the wall of a crumbling, dry well, I cautiously approached the tiny box of a

house. The door was wired shut from outside—positive evidence that no one was there. I hastily untwisted the wire and entered the single small room.

The inside was weirdly dark, considering the time of day. No doubt this was due to the shade of trees all around. I surveyed the contents of the shack: an ancient rocker, a small iron stove, a narrow cot, and wooden crates stacked against the walls for makeshift shelves. The shelves were packed with canned food and battered housewares, as well as the old man's few belongings, which all looked like dump salvage.

Among the store of food and utensils, I ferreted an old Atlas mason jar with a glass cap held on by a rusty clamp. Through the green-tinged glass I beheld an array of triangular, square, and circular coins, each of shining gold.

To remember my younger days shames me now, for this would not have been the first act of thievery I had committed. This time I was caught, and occurrences from that day forward changed my attitude toward the world and myself. It may not have become an altogether better attitude—I cannot say. But at least my preoccupations began to lean elsewhere than toward stealing and bullying.

Old man Keplemann was sitting in the rocking chair below the sack-curtained window when I turned with the intended loot. I hadn't heard him enter, yet he couldn't have been there all along unless I was blind and he could wire doors shut on the outside while sitting on the inside.

I was so taken by surprise at his inexplicable presence that I dropped the antique jar. It shattered on the warped planks. Coins rolled everywhere. Some fell between the cracks of the floorboards.

It wouldn't have been beyond my morals at that age to beat the old man senseless and gather the coins. But something in Keplemann's calm demeanor made me wary. Bullies are by nature cowards, if uncertain of the advantage.

Keplemann began to rock back and forth, back and forth. The rickety piece of furniture creaked and complained. Eerily, when Keplemann rocked back, his head was shadowed in the corner and he looked as young or younger than myself. When he rocked forward into the narrow stream of light from the mostly covered window, he looked even older than his many years. I stood and gaped as he rocked backward toward youth, forward to old age, and back to his youth once more.

"Pick them up if you want them," he said, his voice showing no anger.

"I don't want them," I replied shakily. "I was only looking at them."

Inside short, unkempt whiskers a smile grew, hinting at an understanding of human nature that only the aloofness of a hermit's life can reveal to the conscious psyche. "Have you ever seen their like before?" he asked, whispering as though his question was a secret, sinister riddle.

"You spent some at Mr. Adams's grocery," I answered

with a shrug, trying to put on a show of disinterest. "I saw those."

"Then has *he* seen their like before?" I didn't answer, so the old man continued, rocking all the while and hardly looking at me when he spoke, as though he were only thinking out loud and not really noticing me at all. "No, no, he hasn't, and likely never will again, unless from me. He thinks they're fake coins. Told me so. Says it used to be common for people to mint commemorative medallions in gold or silver, but they weren't really money. I never told him no different. No need to, long as he knows it's worth something anyway."

Here his eyes did finally find me in his room. His gaze was piercing. "There's more, you know, son. Lots more. I'm too old to get it now. But you, now—ah! You! You're young. Strong. You could bring back more. You'd like that, wouldn't you? To be wealthy?"

Frightened by his demeanor, I stumbled past him and out the door. Moments later I was far away on my roaring dirt bike, shaking like a wet pup. Yet my curiosity had been captured. I knew even as I fled in terror of that strange old man that I would come back, and he would be waiting.

In the following days, I could no longer play the game of bully. It was no longer in me. I could only moon over the enigmatic offer.

Often I'd glimpse the old man in his rags off in the distance, leaning on a gnarled stick that served as cane, standing, looking my way. His stance and expression gave no overt invitation. But in my mind, if nowhere else, my manhood was being challenged. He was daring me to some deed. He had stripped me of my lording facade, revealing a young man afraid to go unnoticed and more afraid to be no more important than any other member of a vast and valueless human race. I recognized these thoughts as my own psychosis. Still, it remained singularly important to prove myself to this one woodland vagrant before all others.

Strangely, this man had come to embody both a threat and a salvation. He had offered me riches, but that was merely a ploy, I knew. More obtusely, he had offered the opportunity of rare adventure, a deed at which only a strong young man might hope to succeed, and a chance to prove to myself that I was neither the unimpressive bully always into mischief, nor the coward who fled from an old vagrant's presence.

I had to demonstrate my bravery in the eyes of that useless tramp whose opinion oughtn't to matter. I don't know why, but it seemed to me that if I failed, I'd live forever with self-denigration.

My fear did not abate, but it gave in against my pride and curiosity. I rode up the damp trails through the spruce woods I had of late avoided. The door of the squalid shack was ajar. At first this invitation seemed odd, but the motorbike would have announced my coming well in advance.

He was sitting in that rocker as though he had never

left it, rocking slowly. The light was different and I did not have to suffer the eerie sight of his seeming to age and rejuvenate rhythmically. I sat down on an upturned crate beside a mildew-smelling cot piled with dirty, moth-eaten army blankets. We took up our conversation almost where it had last left off.

I broke into reckless chatter. "Even if the coins are real, they couldn't have belonged to pirates, as some say. There were pirates here, sure, but not so long ago that chests of ancient coins could be uncovered the way they've been found on the Atlantic seaboard and in Europe. Here, the pirates dealt in whiskey and goods, and what gold they stole, they spent. Besides, those gold coins aren't early Canadian or American anyway, so…"

He held up his hand to quiet my nervous prattling and said, "I knew you'd do your homework."

I said no more. I could say nothing he didn't know. He alone had the answers. I didn't even have the right questions.

"I was the pirate," he announced, breaking the silence between us.

"You?"

He nodded, smiling at some reminiscence.

"But not on the waters of the Pacific," he continued, "nor in Puget Sound, nor near the straits. Nor anywhere else you might find on a map. Would you care to know on what waters I did my pirating?"

I sat on the edge of the crate, eyes wide, and waiting. Aloofness was beyond my acting capabilities. I was not so far out of childhood that an improbable story should fail to grip me in suspense.

He leaned toward me and spoke hoarsely. "Below the earth."

I blinked once.

"Below the earth," he repeated more quietly, settling back in his old chair. He grew very still then, his chest rising slowly and falling. His eyes closed to a crack.

I waited a spell, but he made no sign of movement. In a while, I called lowly, "Mr. Keplemann?" A minute later, I shook his shoulder. He was deep in the sleep of the aged. I crept quietly out and closed the door, pushing my trail bike a long way down the path before starting.

Thinking over this second important meeting, it seems a bit ludicrous that I should have been so profoundly affected. I should have dismissed the old hermit as mad, the way most people did. But I wanted to accept his statements, for what reasons I could never fully grasp or rationalize.

In a class at school, the topic seemed to work into the geography lesson we were having, so I asked if underground oceans were plausible. I was searching covertly for solidity on which to hinge the suggestions of the hermit. To my surprise, I received a portion of the explanation I sought.

The geography teacher explained, in reply, that below

midwestern Canada and America, a vast underground ocean did indeed exist, providing, in fact, the major water supply for many regions that lacked lakes or mountains. That ocean was rapidly shrinking because midwesterners were using the water at an alarming rate, faster than it could be naturally replenished. The topic trailed off into a general discussion about water resources, but my own mind wandered onto independent roads.

It was scientifically feasible that a great cavity existed far below Vancouver Island, perhaps beneath the very Pacific—a sea like the sea below the center of the North American continent. It might be deep below granite, undetectable by current technology, or it might simply have gone undiscovered and untapped because the Northwest had such large surface water resources.

I visited Keplemann often after that, and we became close. I called him Sam and soon forgot he'd once been "old man Keplemann, the crazy hermit" to me. But for the longest time he didn't volunteer new information about his mysterious ocean beneath the land. We talked of ordinary matters.

I was not exactly impatient, but I did crave further evidence of that ocean where Sam had been a pirate. So I did some quiet research, unbeknownst to him.

Several days earlier, I'd noticed one of the gold coins wedged between two floorboards. While Sam went outside for a chunk of spruce to throw in his iron stove, I produced my pocket knife and quickly dug the coin out of the floor. I intended only to borrow it, for my malleable character was already being reshaped by the inherent honesty of that lonely man. I hadn't as yet recognized this change in myself.

I mailed the coin to an organization in Montreal that specialized in identifying rare coins. A month passed before I received a letter stating the coin could not be identified by their experts. They were even uncertain whether it was a genuine antique or something minted in the last fifty years. They further stated that its authenticity was highly doubtful, but they could not make any judgment with certainty. They finished their uninformative letter with the offer of an astounding sum of money—quite a price for gold in those days, and far more than should have been bid for any object of dubious authenticity. I refused the offer and eventually the coin was sent to me by registered mail. I returned it secretly to Sam.

Simultaneously, I was trying to get information from a University of British Columbia language professor. I had carefully copied the coin's complex calligraphy and sent it off with a letter. When I received no reply, I wrote a second inquiry. The professor's response came in the form of a curt postcard reading simply, "I don't appreciate jokes."

All this I did without my parents' knowledge. In fact, they were never aware of my friendship with the hermit. They were used to my being off somewhere on my bike, and it had been so long since I'd been in trouble that they were too relieved to ask what I was doing with my time.

After months of avoiding the topic, Sam again became nostalgic for his pirate days, real or imagined. I recall that he had not been feeling well that day. He lay in his dirty bedding, drawing shallow breaths. He spoke sadly but lovingly of the underground sea.

I listened, rapt, to how he first came to the sea by a cavern. The cave was later destroyed by industrial dynamite, trapping Sam in that underground world, he feared, forever. He described vividly the land of darkness and sea. His only light source was a type of ephmerid dayfly that glowed as do lightning bugs. Sometimes they were thick as gnats, creating the illusion of twilight. Other times they were so scarce they had to be captured singly and sealed in lamp jars to be carried about.

His careful descriptions of the stygian sea enchanted me. He told of his first voyage on a boat made of an inverted, gigantic mushroom cap; he nearly died of starvation upon that journey, having nothing to eat but the boat that supported his weight, and a single bizarre crayfish he caught in his bare hands from the freshwater ocean; his salvation came on a day when one more bite from the mushroom craft could only have sunk the vessel, and the choice was to starve or drown.

In that moment of certain death, an ebony island rose out of the eternal night—an isle populated by people the size and stature of penguins. He arrived not as Gulliver, but as a savior—for the penguin people were beset by giants that might well have been Darwin's missing link.

Sam, a greater giant than the troglodytes, staggered from the sea, half drowned, strands of black seaweed dragging from shoulder to foot. He must have seemed to be an aqueous ghoul to the primitive humans who were wreaking havoc on the village of small folk. The troglodytes fled in terror of that coughing, choking specter. After the penguin folk overcame their initial terror, they realized their savior was in need of help himself. It was only a matter of days before he was venerated, veritably, as a protecting god.

As Sam told me this and other fairylike sagas of his netherworld adventures, I would smile or laugh or weep with sorrow. I found myself unable to doubt his fantastic tales. I believed him as thoroughly as he believed himself.

His rather whimsical-appearing penguin followers, he said, had a superior intellect, despite the simplicity of their village lives. At his direction, they built for their godlike hero a black-masted ship of his own design. A select crew of the tiny race sailed with Sam in search of a passage to the surface. "Surface" was a previously unknown concept and, because of a severe language barrier, Sam was never quite able to convey the exact nature of his personal quest. The explorations were readily adapted into the small folks' simple religion, however, as they apparently believed they were looking for heaven with the aid of a fallen deity.

The small folks' quest met constant interference from

the sub-earth country's other race. The troglodytes plagued the more diminutive islanders. Though barely seeming human, the dreaded race had a barbaric civilization of sorts. They built longboats and explored the vast sea, setting up colonies on any island where hunting was good. Part of their diet consisted of the penguin folk, whom the troglodytes considered delicacies and all the more rewarding for the chase provided. The small race lived in fear of extermination.

Sam confessed to me that he had obtained a degree of satisfaction in being worshipped. There was not much else worth his time in that dark land where the sky was made of stone and the stars were flying insects and there was never a guiding constellation. So as all gods are obliged to do, Sam felt a responsibility to aid the faithful lest they be driven to extinction.

His search for passage to the surface, then, was no idle cruise. Along the route of his voyages, Sam and his band of minuscule marauders returned terror with terror, pillaging the coasts of the enemy. Many longboats were sunk by his direction. He taught the penguinlike race the use of bow and arrow, the bows made from the slender backbones of incandescent squids, the arrows fashioned from the spines of subterranean sea urchins. For the first time in the history of that land, the clubs and spears of the troglodytes were of small avail. At last, the greater size of the foe was no advantage.

As in all legends, the Gift of God doesn't arrive without cost. Even Sam hadn't known what price would be paid. Military advances are easily mimicked, and soon the enemy had arrows, too. Thus, Sam had to help his devotees devise a greater weapon: the catapult. Even as the small people constructed it, Sam feared he had begun a cycle that would never stop until one race or the other was driven beneath the sea.

God saw his people die. It pained him to meet them in every harbor and hear their unintelligible prayers for peace. He had never mastered their high-pitched tongue; nor had they been able to learn what was to them the supernatural rumble of Sam's language, a holy speech beyond mortals such as they. Still, communication was quite possible. Sam learned to read their expressions, which more and more often showed pain and unhappiness.

Sam no longer wished to be God.

The day inevitably came. His black-masted ship met an unexpected armada of primitive longboats. The penguin folk stood their posts, the sound of conch horns filling the darkness as arrows flew to and fro. The penguin folk had become the better military tacticians and were still the only race with catapults. Fiery balls were unleashed, some to hiss into inky waters, some to set their targets ablaze. But the troglodytes' armada could not be defeated by a single ship, no matter how superior its design or skilled its crew. The suicidal host could not be forced back. One longboat, set aflame, kept its barbarian crew; oars drove the dragon-faced figurehead into the side of the masted ship, crippling it, sinking it.

In the aftermath, only Sam lived, for the enemy was superstitious and feared to slay the legendary hero who had floundered in the water. They fled, leaving him in the sea surrounded by the flotsam of a broken ship and the drowned corpses of slain little friends.

The chill sub-land winds began to rage as they periodically and mysteriously would do. Sam thought at first that death in cold waters would be welcome. But his will to survive suppressed apathy or depression. In the distance he heard the lapping of water, as against a shore, the sound carrying over the water's surface from miles away. He discerned a whistling as though wind were passing through tunnels. These were sounds of hope; for he had long suspected the inexplicable gales below the stone sky were caused by temperature changes on the surface of the earth, or changes in atmospheric pressure, sucking air in and out as would a bellows. The sound could be nothing less than undiscovered caverns!

Sam salvaged a small fortune by stripping the floating carcasses of their many golden medals, which told of rank and brave errands. Pressed on by the noise of those winds, which more and more seemed to be rushing down, down through many musical caves and tunnels, he righted a lifeboat. With a broken board, he paddled toward the distant sounds. Intermittently, he blew a conch shell he'd salvaged, and listened for the echo, by which he judged the distance between himself and what to the penguin folk was the end of the world.

He came eventually to huge pillars set in a row. They stretched out of the sea and joined the ceiling. Beyond these, he came to a shore rather than the usual abrupt wall. Stalactites hung above dry land, dimly outlined by the lilac light of the ephemerids. Taking the small sack of gold and a container of water dipped from the brineless sea, and the conch shell as an afterthought, he ventured up into the caverns. By chance or destiny he came to the light, which, after so many years, had become alien to his eyes. It was as though he had walked out of a dream; already he could not recall if it had been pleasant or nightmarish.

After this story, Sam had me fetch for him a box kept on a high shelf. He told me to open it. Within was a hideously shaped shell whose spined appearance rendered me afraid to touch it, lest it leap to life and stab me poisonously. It might have been carved from the blackest obsidian by the hand of a mad artist on the sea.

Living as I did near an ocean, I'd seen many queer shells and more than a single giant octopus, but nothing so strange as this. At Sam's prodding, I overcame my dread and raised the tip to my lips and blew into it. A weird, sardonic note resulted—a sound that would have sent wolves fleeing to their dens. I placed the strange souvenir on Sam's chest, and he fell asleep with it. I slipped out silently, leaving him to his needed rest, surprised by the lateness of the hour.

How sad it must be, I thought, for a god to live out his last years as an outcast among his own kind. I began to realize why Sam had befriended me, allowed me to break through the barriers of his hermit's existence. Although his reasons had been selfish, I'd come to love that man, and I would, when asked, help him to return to the place where he was revered, where his death would be a time of mourning rather than a burden to the society that would have to provide a pauper's grave.

Because of various responsibilities, I was unable to visit the hills that week. Sam had lived among the spruces since I was a child. He was so self-reliant that it never occurred to me, as it should have, that his staying in bed during my last long visit was more than a sign of feeling a bit poorly.

One night I awoke hearing the mournful bay of a beast neither cat nor wolf, and knew it to be the conch horn. At that moment, I realized Sam might have gotten worse. I dressed and crept from the nighted house, starting my bike when I was far enough from home that my folks wouldn't hear me go. Little did I know I would never return, or I might have left some cryptic message telling my parents not to worry.

Soon I was to the shanty and at Sam's side. He lay

wheezing with the exertion of blowing the conch. He was pale and sick. I suspected pneumonia.

I started to rush for help, but Sam called me back. He would not let me protest and insisted I help him outside.

"I can make it," he said. "There's time. If you'll help me. The way begins...there!"

He pointed to a dry well. I helped him climb into it, sliding after him down the bucket's sturdy rope. "Never was any water in this here well," he said, laughing feebly. The sound echoed into the well's interior. "I merely disguised the opening." He showed me where to push away rocks leading to a cavern chamber. I held the kerosene lamp in first. A natural, uneven stairway led seemingly into black eternity.

We began the long descent. Sam dropped something from his coat: the conch. I picked it up and carried it for him. He leaned on me as we trekked for hours. He assured me all the while, "It isn't far. It isn't far," but we'd already gone a long, long way. I began to fear there was nothing ahead but death by sickness and starvation, for Sam and me respectively. Sam seemed so certain of the way, but the cavern grew more and more vast, wider, with stony growths cast up and hanging down everywhere.

Our lantern burned low. Measuring the amount of kerosene left, I knew I had not misjudged the amount of time we'd been walking. Sam was so sick I don't know how he kept walking; somehow he persevered.

Down and down we went; and then the lamp's fuel gave out and we stood unmoving in the darkness.

"We can go no farther, Sam," I said, my voice defeated. "We can't see a thing."

Sam's voice replied monstrously in the black hollow of the earth. "Wait. See."

Ever so slowly my eyes began to adjust. What I at first took to be phosphenes—images of light dancing across my retina—coalesced into lilac-colored insect phosphorescence. I left the useless lantern behind, and helped Sam farther down the steep incline. Just as I was ready to give up all hope and admit that we'd become lost in an ordinary cavern, we came to more or less level ground. Before us stretched a tideless ocean. It was shimmering black and reflected the starlike pin dots of light hovering beneath the high roof of the world.

My eyes were not yet so keenly adjusted that I could see much in the darkness. Yet far out on the sea I vaguely perceived the unlikely visage of a sea monster, risen indistinctly out of the inky waters. Sam clenched my hand with his and said the figurehead was from the troglodytes' longboat. Beyond, he saw what I could not: a ship of the penguin folk with masts black as the sky. It was in fast pursuit of the longboat, Sam told me. I didn't know whether or not to believe his description until I saw a comet of flame leave the catapult of the farther ship and streak toward the dragon's head!

The spectacle excited Sam so much that what strength he had left was sapped from him. I held him tight in my left arm, so that he could remain standing to witness the rest.

"As I feared," he whispered hoarsely. "There is still war. Someone needs to stop the clock I set in motion!" He looked at me hopefully when he said this, but I was captivated by the sight on the ocean and didn't catch his full meaning. He murmured, I thought out of fevered irrationality, "After the God of War comes the Prince of Peace."

I watched the huge red flame reflecting on the mirror surface of the water. The dragon head of the longboat was caught in the midst of that bright flame, screaming with the voice of troglodytes. "What a sight!" I said, looking at Sam's face next to mine. But my delight ebbed, for his thin, frail body had gone limp and I knew he was dead. I held him tighter and cried, for I knew for the first time that Sam hadn't been selfish after all. He had not befriended me merely to help him in his final venture. Rather, he had chosen me as heir.

As the enemy longboat sank beneath the dark waters, I raised the conch horn to my lips and beckoned the victors of the battle. Then I gathered Sam's corpse up in both arms and held him like a baby, wondering what adventures awaited me, after the funeral ceremonies for the god-hero I'd brought home to rest.

# THE WEIRD EPISTLES
## OF PENELOPE PETTIWEATHER,
## NORTHWEST GHOST HUNTER

# SERENE OMEN OF DEATH IN THE PIKE PLACE MARKET

*Penelope Pettiweather*
*Seattle, Washington USA*

*Cyril Nettelbaum*
*Ouks, Westbourneshire, England*

Dear Cyril,

Your query to me, "What is the best-known ghost in your city?" might have been answered twenty years ago, "None other than the Burnley School Ghost!" But nowadays the answer would have to be the ghostly

Indian maiden at the Pike Place Sanitary Market, which many a tourist has heard about, and many a market worker has seen.

There are actually several spirits haunting the Market. Rick Mann, for a long time considered "the keeper of the legends"—an eccentric who attended yard sales in a big black hearse—once told a *Seattle Times* columnist, "You really have to wonder if the whole place isn't haunted." He spoke of the "Fat Lady Ghost," a woman of about three hundred pounds who fell through the rotting floor of a café balcony, landing on a table of the main floor. She was spotted a few times after her whimsically grisly demise, but no lasting tradition grew up around her.

A volunteer worker at Left Bank Books admitted to me that she no longer stayed in the shop after closing. She had once heard someone's slow, plodding, inexplicable footsteps moving back and forth in the upstairs room, though absolutely no one but herself was in the store. This may have been the same spirit seen a few years ago in an upper-floor restaurant that was called Vitium Capitale. The ghost was observed by a Samoan cook, who often opened or closed the restaurant alone. The figure stood before the beautifully multipaned windows, gazing down at the Market, or across the roof of the main Market building to where the ferries were plainly visible. This spirit was an exceedingly tall black youth with dreadlocks, gaunt and morosely handsome. Another café has taken over the same location, up the staircase from Left Bank Books. No one who presently works there has seen the watchful spirit, so perhaps he has traveled onward or upward.

Two ghosts haunt the Market's bead store. The famed Indian maiden drops by at three-month intervals. The other is a lonely, somewhat mischievous, and surprisingly lively ghost who dwells in the store pretty much constantly. Lynn Roberts Hancock of the Craft Emporium and Bead Shop said, "The first time I knew he was there was when he came and did this," and she demonstrated by pulling on columnist Rick Anderson's sleeve.

One day, the spirit turned on her radio, for ghosts are frequently able to influence radios, record players, and taping devices—perhaps the intangibility of "sound" is something their own intangibility can most easily deal with. Hancock said, "I turned it off. He turned it back on. I unplugged it, *and it still played*. Then we put it in a box, *and it still played*. Then we put the box with the radio in it in a drawer. *It still played.*"

The ghost displays a great deal of personality. Once a very obnoxious customer had a small plastic fruit tossed at her. Hardly "mean-spirited," but it got a point across. Hancock made some lame and hasty excuse that things were always falling off the ceiling, but the customer knew something was amiss. The ghost clearly felt a degree of proprietorship and didn't think his "employee" ought to be harassed by unreasonable people.

Occasionally the shop's ghost gets a little out of hand, knocking things awry or pulling stunts like that with the radio. These events seem to occur whenever he has been overlooked for a long time. He acts up to gain attention and, having achieved it, settles down for a while. Hancock said, "I've adjusted. I am very comfortable with him these days."

The best-known and longest-persisting Market ghost is definitely the Indian maiden. She was reported throughout the 1950s and many times since; she was probably seen in earlier decades as well, but I have not found a surviving record of it. By various witnesses' reports, she is sometimes transparent, sometimes more substantial but with a white light about her, and sometimes so tangible that she is taken for an ordinary living woman. When spoken to, she vanishes. Her hair is in braids that fall to her waist. She wears a floor-length dress and a shawl that was once brightly colored, but now faded from long use.

Most reports claim she is in her twenties, but at least one person observed her to be elderly, with brown, crinkly skin. All agree her appearance is one of regal serenity, even beatitude. A relatively recent addition to her lore is that her name is Princess Angeline and she is the daughter of Chief Sealth, for whom our city is named.

This identification is only recently grafted onto this ghost, and I don't personally think it has much validity.

Princess Angeline lived to a regal, beautiful old age and saw the town named for her father become a real city. In the early days of the now-lamented Frederick and Nelson store, which was then on Second Avenue, Indians sat outside the store selling woven blankets and such. But Angeline was far too noble for such activity, which is why I reject the late-occurring legend that the Pike Place Indian Maiden is Angeline.

Even in her lifetime, folk memory held that Angeline had, in her youth, saved the city from an Indian attack. If this was untrue, she never corrected anyone, for it had become a tradition that the favor be returned to her, and many of the shop owners were in agreement that all her needs were to be met for her entire life. In consequence, she would go into Frederick's and similar stores and carry out as much as her arms could hold of fancy foods, knick-knacks, and dresses. In consequence her house became jam-packed with wonderful and useless possessions. That's the real Princess Angeline, and I cannot see room in her history to account for her appearing as a young ghostly maiden.

By older tradition, which we may regard as better evidence, the ghost lived in the early part of this century, when the Market was first established. In those days, she was one of the many independent merchants. She sold handmade baskets and several witnesses have reported that when she appeared, she was carrying her baskets. As the story goes, she vanished suddenly, and no one ever knew what became of her.

In 1983, Rick Anderson interviewed a man named Leon, who at the time purported to be the last living individual to have seen the Indian maiden. There were actually many sightings after Leon's 1963 experience, but not everyone at the Market compares notes on these matters. Leon had a gift shop on the Market's lower level. In those days, most sightings of the Indian woman were on or near the ramp leading to a branch of Goodwill Industries, which rented one of the largest spaces in the Market. The ghost was also known to pass straight through walls, apparently adhering to corridors that alterations of the Market's configuration had closed off or eradicated.

Leon was standing in the hallway with three other shopkeepers when the ghost passed right by them on her way to the Goodwill ramp. She looked like a normal person to Leon, but the others were very startled by her. One of his fellow merchants said, "That's her. That's the ghost."

"Pshaw," said Leon, and separated from his friends immediately in an effort to catch the woman and prove her to be tangible. He had not followed very far when she vanished in the blink of an eye. Leon still couldn't believe it, and went so far as to ask a woman to check the ladies' bathroom to see if the Indian maiden was somewhere about. "But she just wasn't there," Leon afterward admitted. "I'd seen her walk by my shop before. Although she seemed somewhat odd, moving slowly as if her feet barely touched the floor, and never turned her head, I hadn't thought much about her. She seemed perfectly human. She was rather large, with grayish black hair. But when I really thought about it, she *had* always been strange. Her long dress changed colors in a mysterious way, first lavender, then pink."

There had long been a belief that all who saw the serene Indian maiden were destined for a violent death, though not necessarily right away. Informant Rick Mann reported that it was extremely unlucky to see her. Of the three people who were with Leon on the day he tried to catch up with the ghost, he said, "Bill had a heart attack. Marie committed suicide. And Ruth was murdered." As for Leon, Rick Anderson tried a few years later to do a follow-up interview—and discovered Leon was missing. His fate remains unknown.

Reporter Paul Andrews investigated the Market ghosts in October of 1983 for *Pacific Magazine*, and found that most people believed the Indian woman made her rounds frequently, but only after the lights were out and the Market closed for the night, or she would be seen even more often. For all the bustle, noise, and color of the Market's working hours, it does close early, and becomes a series of gloomy, windswept semi–open-air hallways, sectioned by chain gratings on the upper level, by fire doors on the lower. There is limited access even for merchants, and few would ever have the chance to see the maiden and to fall under her sorrowful curse.

No one actually believes she is malignant, because she appears so beatific. Supposedly, those doomed to deaths as tragic as her own are more susceptible to seeing her, but she in no way causes their fates. Many people have observed her and are alive to tell of it—but since there is no time limit on the purported curse, they could live to be ninety, die of pneumonia or in a car accident, and blame the death on the maiden.

I for one never believed she was malignant, or I would not have made the effort I made to communicate with this spirit. I had every expectation of coming face to face with her, and no fear of dropping dead as a result. I worked one summer at Shakespeare and Company Books on one of the lower levels of the Market, and often had occasion to stay late, eagerly awaiting her presence.

I talked to many fellow marketeers about the maiden. Those who bore witness to her existence were not really scared they were doomed for having seen the beautiful spirit, but they were aware of the past deaths and often had little twinges of worry.

After the Goodwill closed its Market branch and that space was renovated, the Indian maiden began to haunt another inside level. She took a special liking to Lynn Hancock's bead store, which is down a dead-end corridor, with windows overlooking Puget Sound. Lynn said, "She was standing back there looking at seed beads. I walked back and said, 'May I help you?' and she was gone. It was like she was never there."

After the Indian disappeared, Hancock was shaken enough to close her store. She stood outside near the rest room and wondered if she had hallucinated. "I thought I'd been working too hard." But it happened again, and other workers in the shop spotted the ghost as well. Because of the fear that surrounded her appearance—the purported violent deaths that followed sightings—Hancock was taking no chances. An Indian shaman was brought in to put a Circle of Protection around the bead store. "He had an eagle-feather fan and sage and sweet grass. Both my kids were here, and we went through the ceremony."

Protective sage hangs in the shop to this day. If that spectral Indian maiden ever was really the source of dangerous curses, the efforts of the knowledgeable medicine man have surely restrained the ill effects of seeing her. The ghost continued to appear in three-month cycles, and Lynn personally observed her a half-dozen times in the following years. Never again were untoward deaths credited to the maiden's appearance, and what could be more sweetly touching than a ghost's continued interest in Indian seed beads?

One night I stayed late in the bookshop to organize shelves. It had been a hot summery day, and the south wing of the lower level held the muggy heat all evening. I was on a high ladder alphabetizing sundry titles; up near the ceiling, the heat was even more unbearable. Yet without preamble, I felt a sudden chill, and immediately climbed down from the ladder to see if the fire door exit had been opened by someone, though it was supposed to be locked after hours.

I found it was indeed still locked. Where had the cool draft come from?

I looked south along the darkened corridor and saw a faint glow moving away. I hurried after it. The light was blue shifting to lavender. "Hello!" I called, but the shimmering Indian woman did not look back. I called again, "Wait!" and my voice echoed in the empty corridor. She moved steadily but slowly, and I was closing on her. She went up the staircase to the next level of the Market. I hurried up the stairs and saw that she was heading up the ramp toward the Sound View Café, holding a basket in her arms.

I focused all my attention upon her, knowing she was apt at any time to vanish. I was trying to "hold her fast," as one tries to hold on to a dream upon waking. By this method I was able to keep her in sight. She went right by the Sound View and started down another stairway. The steps were wide enough that I could walk right beside her. She was oblivious to my presence.

We came to the back entry of the day-care center, which is in part of the old Goodwill space. She walked straight through a closed doorway. It was locked after hours, so I could no longer follow, and felt a terrible sense of loss that this was so.

I peered through a small glass window and saw her striding down the slanted floor. I sent my thoughts after her, trying my hardest to establish some communication—and briefly, I succeeded. She stopped, turned slowly, and gazed at me through the glass.

In her gaze, I felt engulfed by overwhelming serenity. I experienced a sense of reassurance such as I can never describe. She then showed me the contents of her basket, which was a pure light. In that moment she had ceased to be an Indian maiden, for she had herself become part of the pure light. Out of that brightness there issued—how can I say it? I was so profoundly affected, I thought surely I was viewing a manifestation of Divine Love, and really wondered if I weren't in the presence of a Goddess.

Then the light was gone. Nothing of the ghost remained, and I was panting with a kind of desire to possess that light.

As you well know, Cyril, I am no novice when it comes to hauntings. But this one really was different. I hardly dare try to make sense of it. Had I been in China, I would have sworn I'd been visited by Kuan Yin, Goddess of Compassion. As it is, she will always be an enigma to me. All I know is that even now, when I think of her basket full of light, all the sad feelings of life are shunted

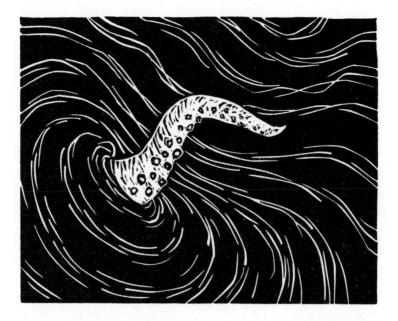

# The
# Forest
# in the Lake

*Penelope Pettiweather*
*Seattle, Washington USA*

*Cyril Nettelbaum*
*Ouks, Westbourneshire, England*

Dear Cyril,

Why, of course, when you make your journey from your beloved shires of England to the equally misty Pacific Northwest of America, I will certainly house you. What sort of friend would your old Penelope be otherwise? There's no sense spending extravagant fees at a bed and breakfast when you've a friend in the vicinity. As for your overly cautious fretting over what my neighbors might say about me if an old English bachelor spent a week or so with an old American bachelorette—well, Cyril, to tell the truth, it rather appeals to me that any neighbor of mine could actually suppose, after all these years, I've finally gotten up the nerve to become an old sinner.

The "true" legends you recounted to me in your last letter, regarding British lake monsters, were delightful, and they have gone straight into my "collection" of strange-but-true accounts of haunted or strangely inhabited water-ways the world over. You're quite right. The Northwest has its share of traditional beasties of a similar type, dwelling along the ocean's coast, the Strait of Juan de Fuca, Puget Sound, and in every lake hereabouts. In Lake Steilacoom near Tacoma, the evil Whe-atchee, a female monster, dwells under the water, so that the Nisqually Indians refused to fish or swim there. Fish Lake near Mount Adams had a dragon in it that hid behind a door in the bed of the lake. The Klickitat Indians would not eat fish from that lake and shunned it generally. Rain spirits dwelt in all the lakes be-tween Mount Adams and Mount Rainier, these being benevolent and respected; but the rain spirits hated noise and if their quietude was disrupted, the next rain would be an awful storm.

A serpent monster big enough to swallow canoes in

Lake Quinault on the Olympic Peninsula did battle with the heroic figure Kwatee the Changer. Spirit Lake near Mount St. Helens was the abode of numerous evil spirits, and Indians rarely hunted near it, claiming they heard demonic noises in the lake—which obviously was the rumbling of that very active volcano. The Spirit Lake monsters were called Seatco and were known to drag fishermen to the bottom. A ghost elk was credited with luring hunters to Spirit Lake so the Seatco could get them, for the Indian method of hunting was to drive elk into the water. One creature dwelling there was an enormous fish with a bear's head and it ate people. There are literally hundreds of stories like these!

But some of the strange tales of the Great Northwest's aquatic oddities are not legends at all, but bold facts of science that *ought* to be legends even when they aren't.

For instance, the biggest octopi in the world are not found in the depths of the Indian Ocean or in some other faraway tropical waters. They're right here in Puget Sound. Scuba divers say the giant octopus is a whimsical fellow who likes to play—shy at first, but very trusting and curious if given the chance. Some of these clever beasties have learned that divers thrash about in a most wonderful and entertaining manner if the octopus entwines itself in the diving gear and commences to disconnect the hoses. When an octopus "laughs," the colors shift along its body, just like a blushing person.

The intelligence of these creatures was suggested by a half-grown and very friendly octopus who lived at the old Seattle Aquarium. This was back in the days of the famed Namu and other killer whales. In those days the aquarium was certainly not the state-of-the-art affair it is today. It had a quaint sideshow atmosphere. Visitors were encouraged to feed the seals bits of fish purchased for the purpose, and a series of short-lived whales in undersized pools were each in turn eager to stick their fins out of the water to "shake hands." Strictly as an aside, I had a crush on a whale called Kandu, and if no one was watching I was able to coax her to me. I actually kissed her snout on several occasions. The tragedy and the beauty of their captive personalities was really very touching. They did so poorly in small pools, it was certainly a good idea to stop capturing them.

Back then the aquarium was located entirely at the end of a pier otherwise taken up by Pirate's Plunder, an import concern. For several weeks the workers were puzzled about what had been happening to their blue crabs. Each time they replenished the supply, the crabs would be picked off mysteriously, a few each night, with only their empty shells left behind. Then one night a worker "caught" a certain octopus, who lived about four tanks away from the crabs, going about one of his midnight sorties. This fellow could squeeze his body out of a surprisingly small hole— far too small, by appearances, for any octopus to get through—and then he crawled across the top of the tanks until he got to the blue crabs' home. He would then squeeze through another small hole, eat a few crabs, and return by the same route, leaving no clue regarding his nightly endeavors. The thing is, when the octopus was finally caught in the act, he made a valiant effort to get out of the blue crab tank and back to his own home as quickly as possible, like a dog caught chewing his master's slippers and striving against all hope to deny his part in it.

Back in the 1970s, the Point Defiance Aquarium in Tacoma used to keep a couple of giant octopi where they could be petted. Because the octopus is so sensitive in captivity, the aquarium no longer does this. Even back then, there was a sign on the pool of each that read, "Do Not Touch the Octopus." But it was impossible not to do so. Those big things were *tame*. They *wanted* you to touch them. How could a visitor resist? And, once again, if you can believe it, these creatures seemed genuinely to love practical jokes.

One octopus would come to the far side of the top of its pool and hang from the rim. It would reach one of its great huge tentacles across the surface toward the clutch of observers, using the very tip of its tentacle like a little finger calling "Come hither." Children and adults alike easily recognized what that motion meant and were tempted to touch the tentacle, but were usually reluctant and tentative about it, for they could never be sure the big monster didn't actually want to eat them.

In fact, the octopus had no intention of hurting anybody. Despite the parrotlike beak in the center of that tangle of arms, it's rare for them to bite even when frightened. That Point Defiance octopus genuinely liked to be petted, and his "come hither" was a seriously intended ploy to gain physical contact with humanity. I suppose it sounds quite fantastic if you've never acquired any knowledge of octopi in the sea or in captivity, but take Penelope's solemn oath, these beasts are as wise and affectionate, in their own way, as anyone's dog or cat. And if you and I were a sea-dwelling merman and mermaid, surely we'd have octopi as our companions.

As weirdly smart as the octopus is, the aquarium's seductive fellow understood full well that people who didn't know its personality were *scared* to touch it even if they were tempted.

Picture if you will the child or adult who slowly, slowly, ever so slowly reaches closer and closer to that "come hither" tentacle. The tentacle, too, moves slowly, slowly—until the human hand touches the water, then *zap!* the octopus reaches out rapidly and grabs the hand! That hand comes out of that pool as fast as lightning, accompanied by a loud yelp of surprise. And the octopus begins to "laugh" its blushing laugh.

I would visit that very octopus at least once a month, and I saw it pull this stunt dozens of times. It clearly knew what it was up to. But whenever somebody failed to jerk away, and wasn't afraid, the octopus was eager to befriend the visitor. It would grab hold of the entire hand, and pull itself to the side of the pool nearest the newfound friend. Its coloration would lighten, and it would grow perfectly calm to be petted.

These octopi recognized their keepers, and liked some of them better than others. They knew who had the food and who didn't, who would play with them and who wouldn't. They also "played" with objects, just as would a cat. Most scientists think octopi are very short-lived in the wild, which is truly sad, because they obviously love life. Out in Puget Sound, they build houses of stones, and prefer to make them from the prettiest rocks. They collect useless objects, especially shiny bits of metal and smoothed glass, to keep in their houses. To tell the truth, I rather relate to their view of the world, living as I do amidst my own accumulation of quaint clutter.

These boneless beasts learn a great deal and store up a lot of knowledge, for they have the ability to "remember" things they're only reminded of occasionally and have no intrinsic need to know. This may all sound fantastic, but every word is true; get any modern octopus book out of your library, and you'll find many things even more remarkable about the animal.

All this tentacled wit and wisdom has to be crowded into a life span of only about seven years. That saddens me quite a bit, for our own lives of seventy or eighty years seem so very short, and here is an animal that delights in its world but lives very briefly indeed. However, some investigators at the University of Washington are now of the opinion that the Puget Sound giant octopus may actually live quite a bit longer than previously supposed; only those that live in captivity succumb quickly.

Yet another "strange but true" bit of Northwest natural history regards the underwater forest in Lake Washington. The lake is not only the largest in western Washington, it happens to be one of the deepest lakes in the United States. It is two hundred feet down in places, with another hundred feet of silt—three hundred feet to solid ground—and exceedingly cold both because of the depth and the water feeding in from the mountain glaciers. Nevertheless, the area of Lake Washington was once a deep valley with no water in it at all, except for some little streams, I suppose.

The shifts that land can make are extremely slow. By increments over thousands or even millions of years, the valley became sealed on all sides, and then filled with water. It happened so slowly that the valley forests adjusted to their new environment! Those "antediluvian" fir forests are still down there, and in a few places from a boat, you can see the tops of the trees reaching for the light, never quite breaking the surface of the water.

One of my uncles—Wilson, not the eccentric Elvin—

was a scuba diver in the navy many years ago. After he left the navy, he taught scuba diving lessons, oh, way back in the sixties and seventies. He was the first person to tell me how some of the octopi in Puget Sound had gotten to "understand" divers and liked to get on top of them and unplug their equipment, just for fun.

Scuba divers don't usually like the lakes, because they're much dirtier than the sea, and it's harder to keep one's equipment cleared of floating plants. But Wilson had heard about the submerged forest and wanted to see it for himself. Soon he was out there in Lake Washington, and though it's a whole lot cleaner than it was a great many years ago when sewage was dumped right into it, you just never get the kind of clarity you do in Puget Sound.

Therefore Wilson was right amidst the forest before he realized it, for the trees had not been visible until he was quite close to them. He was disappointed that the trees were extremely raggedy and not very attractive. Some hardly looked like they were still alive. He swam around several of them. They were gigantic, and their bark was sturdy; they were in no way decayed or rotten. Clearly they *were* still alive, even if their needles were awfully skimpy. Most of the few needles were to be found near the tops of the long trunks.

Then he saw something odd in the shadowy underwater fir forest. There appeared to be a scrap of trawler's net strung between two trees. The net stretched from the silt nearly to the top of the trees to which it was snagged. It almost looked like a spider's web, with eight enormous threads converging on a center. Trawling was illegal in the lake, and Wilson's first thought was that whoever lost this net must have dumped it overboard on purpose when spotted by a patrol boat.

As he approached the strange net, he saw that the great knot in the center was alive. His heart began to palpitate with wonder, for he had been diving long enough to know there were no fleshy creatures like that anywhere in the Northwest, and certainly nothing that made fat, stringy webs! But undeniably one gigantic eyeball was peering at him through the water's haze. Wilson drifted there, gazing back at that enormous eye, until slowly it dawned on him where he had seen just such a sight.

It was the eye of an octopus! But the eight legs, which he had mistaken for some kind of netting, were far too skinny to be those of an ordinary octopus. And although the biggest octopi in the world were in Puget Sound, they did not live in fresh water; and they weren't even half as big as the monster in front of him now.

But if trees could adjust to living under water, then assuredly a special strain of octopus might adapt to fresh water, given thousands of years to evolve. It was feasible that a colony of Puget Sound octopi had been cut off from the Sound ages ago, and, as their salt lake became purified over time by the influx of fresh water, this strain adapted.

They changed over the generations until they were even larger than their giant cousins in the Sound. Their bodies became fatter, their tentacles longer and thinner, like ropes. And if they dwelt in the siltier places of Lake Washington, no one would ever see or catch them in the hundred feet of muck wherein they raised their families.

Wilson knew that it was the nature of octopi to be shy, unless their trust was won, and then the creatures would be friendly and mischievous. They were never dangerous. But this one was so enormous, perhaps it wouldn't behave like a normal octopus. Perhaps he, Wilson, looked like a tasty little morsel! He was torn between his fear and his curiosity. He wanted to swim away as fast as he could, but he also wanted to get nearer the thing to find out if it was truly real.

Kicking his flippers lightly, Wilson glided toward the beastly apparition. The great eye rotated to watch him. Then one of those long, ropy tentacles came loose from the limb to which it had been clinging, and reached for the scuba diver—slowly, slowly, closer and closer. It was not a threatening motion, but indicated curiosity. The coloration changed slowly in waves or bands, like a great dark rainbow of grays and browns and faint pinks rippling through its body.

Just before the tip of the tentacle touched him, Wilson panicked. He thrashed the water to get away from the monster and pulled his diving knife from its strap at his heel. The enormous, spidery octopus responded in kind. All the tentacles came loose from the trees, and seemed to partially retract into the bulbous body. Then with a jet of ink, the creature shot away like a dart.

Too late, Wilson regretted himself. He followed the trail of ink through the water until it faded away, the track leading into the deeper waters where a diver couldn't reach, and toward an area of deep silt.

Wilson explored the area as deep as he dared to go, until his tank was too nearly out of air for him to continue. At one point, he spied a curious arrangement of stones poking up from the silt in one place, causing Wilson to imagine a stone-built "city" under the mud. But he saw no evidence of the creature.

In weeks and months to come, and for several years to follow, he returned again and again to the underwater forest, always taking special camera equipment with him. But never again did a friendly tentacle reach forth in curiosity to welcome the diver.

Thine obediently,<br>
Penelope

# THE
# OVAL
# DRAGON

*Penelope Pettiweather*
*Seattle, Washington USA*

*Jane Bradshaw*
*Oundle, Northants, England*

Dear Jane,

I'm glad you liked that "fish story" (or should I say "octopus story"?), which Cyril put in the last number of his little magazine. Your passing nit about "octopuses" or "octopedes" being the proper plurals, rather than "octopi," is well taken. I can see that a Greek word with a Latin plural would sound odd to a language expert. But to mere Americans, "octopi" has become so common that it sounds right to us, even if it is absurd.

I've been collecting these serpenty tales for some time now (and you thought I only liked ghosts!). So I was delighted to get the added tale of "the squishy thing from the loch" of your experience. You ask if I have personally seen any sea serpents, and I regret to say I have not—not yet, at least. But do remind me I should write you sometime about a gigantic, barnacle-encrusted sea maiden I saw near the Swinomish Reservation.

I've been trying for some while to meet one of these beasties and have based several camping trips on legends I've heard. A lake near the Cascade foothills by Mount Adams was previously ruled by a gigantic swan queen named Hawelakok. She let people use the water from her lake, but stirred it up to drown whoever tried to take fish from it. There are Indian kelpies as well—like the American Lake spotted ghost horse, which grabs swimmers and drowns them.

You ask if anyone here ever "fakes" sea serpents, as is often done in sundry Scottish lochs to draw tourists. To my knowledge, this has never been done locally. Despite a great many lake monster legends in the Northwest, no one has cashed in on them for tourist value. Since *authentic* lore has been for the most part ignored, I suppose there's just no "market" for fakery. I can't recall any incidents such as the event you recount of that group of duffers who actually built an elaborate hoax serpent to troll about in the lake mists. Fishermen certainly do tell whopping tales about things they've nearly captured, but no one has yet reported to me any elaborate hoaxes attendant to their tales. Perhaps most Americans lack the British wit to invent and imagination to believe. On the other hand, we *do* have on the Columbia River a druid style "folly" in the form of a perfect replica of Stonehenge put up by a wealthy eccentric, Sam Hill. He unfortunately didn't have the monument built facing the right direction, so it's useless for equinoctial observances.

In America, I think it is much more common to fake flying saucers than ghosts or lake monsters. I recall in the seventies there was a flying saucer convention here in Seattle, and one evening a couple of good ol' boys let loose some weather balloons with traffic flares dangling off them. About fifty UFO conventioneers had such "believing" mindsets that they were thoroughly convinced they'd shared a mass sighting, until the traffic flare melted part of one of the balloons and it fell amidst them.

I must say, though, that there are some examples of fishermen's lore that do make one pause to wonder. The *usual* point of a good fish story is to credit oneself for nearly bagging the biggest one that ever got away. But even the most inveterate of liars, such as all fishermen are, set limitations on what they feel the listener is gullible enough to believe. The purpose of the lie is altogether lost if the teller seeks anonymity. Even so, the teller of one curious tale, first recorded in the *Tacoma Daily Ledger* way back on July 3, 1893, wished his name not to be revealed, for it was a whale of a tale he might justifiably expect never to be believed.

The fisherman who first told the tale to the *Ledger*'s reporter a century ago was an easterner, which, in those days, was often thought sufficient to explain a lunatic character. He and three other men set out from Tacoma on a three-day fishing tour of the sound. "Our party was supplied with the necessaries of life as well as an abundance of its luxuries," the easterner reported, the "luxuries" including whiskey and rye. He said, "But it must not be inferred from this fact that the luxuries played any part in creating the sights seen on that memorable outing. We left Tacoma on July first, Saturday, about four-thirty in the afternoon and, as the wind was from the southeast, we shaped our course for Point Defiance."

They fished at Point Defiance for a while, then tried their hand at a Henderson Island trout stream that poured into Black Fish Bay, the name "black fish" alluding to the orca whales that visit these waters even today. The geological features of the sea floor are unusual at this location, and the waters in this area are extraordinarily deep.

The men camped the night on the island, having imbibed sufficiently that their wits were undoubtedly a bit dulled. Thus, their ensuing adventure had an edge of drunken unreality about it, and we can only speculate what percentage of their experience was misunderstood by themselves in their varied states of inebriation.

Along about midnight, a frightful noise awoke the four men, a crackling sound accompanied by a stinging sensation, like thousands of little needles stabbing them through their blankets and clothes. This very sensation has in recent times been caused by electrical "leaks" into the ground from high voltage wires, and has caused pets and farm animals to leap straight up from the ground, and cows to stop giving milk or even to be killed. But in 1893, the phenomenon could hardly have been blamed on high voltage wires, there being none on Henderson Island. Had things stopped at this point, we might easily have supposed the little camp had just survived being struck by lightning. Things did not stop at that, but progressed weirdly.

The easterner said, "The air was filled with a strong current of electricity that caused every nerve in the body to sting with pain. A light as bright as that created by a concentration of many arc lights constantly flashed. I turned my head in that direction, and if it is possible for fright to turn a man's hair white, then mine ought to be white now."

Fortunately for him, the easterner still had black hair.

Had the phenomenon been lightning-related, he might well have been rendered bald, for those struck by lightning are known sometimes to lose every hair on their head, never to regrow it.

"There before my eyes," the fisherman continued, "was a most horrible-looking monster. The monster slowly drew in toward shore and, as it approached, its head poured out a stream of water that looked like blue flame."

The amazing story, it might appear, regarded some heretofore unknown species of electric fish, for we may recall that electric eels put out enough current to shock a man to death. The holiday fisherman reported that it was one hundred feet long and thirty feet in circumference. "Its shape was somewhat out of the ordinary insofar as the body was neither round nor flat, but oval. It had coarse hair on the upper body. At about every eight feet from its head to its tail, a substance that had the appearance of a copper band encircled it. Blue flames came from two hornlike structures near the center of the head. The tail was shaped like a propeller."

Now from the "hair" we could suppose either sea algae, which is known to adhere to certain sea animals, or else the oval monster was a mammal. It is perfectly feasible that one hundred years ago, remnants of the once-plentiful giant sea cow, hunted to extinction by whalers, had found its way to Black Fish Bay. As for the horn, the narwhal sports a single horn, and many species of fish and reptile sport one or more horns. The copper bands would seem to be only coloration, a striped animal being common enough, unless we are speaking of something literally metallic that aided in the manufacture or conduction of electricity.

"Sir, I tell you, in the electrically charged atmosphere, birds and insects died. Two of my fellow fishermen became paralyzed when licked by the blue flame. They lay on the beach until they eventually recovered. At last, the monster submerged into the dark waters and a telltale light betrayed its course. I hardly need tell you we were not long getting underway for Tacoma, and I can assure you I may no more desire to fish in waters of this bay. There are too many peculiar inhabitants in them."

When we resort to science, the first response to this story is to say it is an impossibility. Certainly no such animal is known, and if it did once exist, it must now be extinct. Luminous fish, some of monstrous size, are known to students of ocean life. The report of a "furred" quality to the beast reminds us that from Alaska to the Northwest there are many reports of gigantic, long-necked seals, which were the mammalian equivalents of the plesiosaurs. No specialist in the sea will deny that it is filled with species uncatalogued, and occasionally strange beasts have washed ashore on various coasts, decayed by the time scientists investigate, so that the mysteries remain irresolvable.

In the last century and this, there have been many

sightings of such sea creatures in Puget Sound and the Strait of Juan de Fuca. None repeated the features of the Oval Dragon of Point Defiance; none spouted electrified water. If the four men were hoaxed, they were hoaxed well. If they were fully inebriated by their admitted "luxuries," then pray tell, how did they hallucinate the same experience together?

As you can see, Jane, I've pondered this old tale from every possible angle in an attempt to surmise whether or not there is any chance it actually happened as reported. Your account of a loch serpent hoax caused me to think of this old report, and I do wonder if the four fishermen weren't the victims of some dangerous mistake, if not exactly a hoax.

Perhaps the most believable explanation was that the Oval Dragon was actually a mechanical device, such as fascinated Victorians generally. It wouldn't take a mad scientist, but only an eccentric inventor, to build in secret an electrically driven ship shaped generally like a fat serpent. Several elements of the eye-witness description suggest a human contrivance of this sort. The "propeller"-shaped tail may indeed have been a propeller. The two spewing horns may have been exhaust pipes. The copper bands may have been part of a primitive electrical generator. Its mouth, which spewed blue water, may have been only the result of a hand-operated water pump, which had the perfectly utilitarian purpose of keeping the vessel afloat. The very oval fatness of the serpent implies a hull of some sort.

Such a ship might well, like the ironclad monitors built as early as the Civil War, ride so low in the water as to nearly resemble a submarine. And its passenger-inventor would ride inside, unseen by observers and probably unable to see the camping fishermen in the darkness outside the vessel. The act of pumping water out the mouth of the figurehead would have caused the low-riding vessel to lurch upward, and it would certainly be a shocking thing to fishermen who were sleepy and possibly a bit tipsy viewing it in the starlight.

It's only my theory, but I like to envision within the Oval Serpent the passenger-inventor sitting at the controls, like a character out of a Jules Verne novel, pumping water from his electric ironclad. It was a test ride rather than a hoax, but had the same effect. By accident the inventor nearly electrocuted the startled campers.

It's an amusing theory, but it almost demands a sad conclusion. As his invention was never revealed to the world at large, it may well be that he succeeded in electrocuting himself by means of the same electrical discharge experienced by the fishermen even on dry land. He fried himself crisp as a chip inside his ship, which sank in the unnaturally deep waters, never again to be seen—save only by the orcas and the octopi (or octopuses).

Love,
Penelope

# LEGEND OF THE WHITE EAGLE SALOON

*Penelope Pettiweather*
*Seattle, Washington USA*

*Jane Bradshaw*
*Oundle, Northants, England*

My dear Jane,

**C**an you imagine a teetotaler like myself spending a whole evening in a tavern? I'm sure you can—if there's a ghostie or two involved. A little article clipped out of an Oregon paper was handed to me by a friend who knows of my interests. A week or so later I found myself heading down the freeway to Portland. I arrived in the city in the afternoon and, after registering at a favorite bed and breakfast, I spent most of the rest of the day doing my usual library research. Then I headed off to one of Portland's oldest bars, the White Eagle Café and Saloon on North Russell Street.

The music for which the place is famed had not yet started, as it was still rather early. So the room was a lot more conducive to conversation than it would have been with a band. Even so, I'm much more comfortable in a haunted house than in any kind of bar, and I have no experience talking to bartenders. So I shyly took a seat at the far end of the bar and quietly sipped a tomato juice.

The place, all done in mahogany, was surprisingly clean. Only a few people were there, a relatively young and attractive clientele, mostly reading books or newspapers and staying to their own few cubic feet of world. The place did have a comfortable atmosphere overall, and I imagined it must be one of the friendlier places when things were hopping. I nevertheless felt out of place because to my way of thinking, beer tastes like swamp water filtered through moldy bread, wine tastes like cherries left in a sunlit puddle to go sour, and Scotch tastes like cleaning fluid or paint remover. And I always suspected that if tequila was supposed to have a worm in it, then a grasshopper ought to have crickets and katydids.

When the bartender came to my end of the bar to see if I needed a refill of tomato juice, I handed him one of those silly little cards you sent me for Christmas a couple of years ago. You remember—the ones that say, "Penelope Pettiweather, American Ghost Hunter," under a lovely dingbat of a clipper ship. I still have some of them because I usually feel too embarrassed handing them out. But this time it seemed an icebreaker. The bartender laughed and introduced himself as Chad Hayes, proprietor. He had a wise, owlish look. I imagined him not running a bar day in and day out, but out in the woods with a tent and a Coleman lantern and a dozen good books.

We talked for a while, and I took notes. Then he said, "There's someone you really should meet." He made a quick phone call and returned to where I was sitting. "We got lucky. Joan was home and says she needs something to do anyway."

"Who's Joan?" I asked.

"She owned the place in the sixties. Those two ghosts were hanging around here even back then!"

"So there really are two?" I inquired. We'd only been talking about a ghost called Sam, but the article I'd read had indeed mentioned a second ghost.

"Yeah, Sam drank himself to death, near as I can figure, unless he shot himself in the head. His girl was named Rose. They lived upstairs in separate apartments back in the twenties or thirties. Some of the rooms still served as a brothel. I've heard Rose weeping in the early hours, after the rock bands go home and the place is shut up and quiet. I don't know if she killed herself or was killed by Sam, but when she starts sobbing, she sounds awfully unhappy about something."

Chad wandered away to serve his patrons, but business was still pretty slow, so he wandered back to me. He picked up where he left off. "Yeah, it used to give me the creeps, but I've gotten used to it. This place was awfully violent back in those days, so what can you expect with a history like that? Do you know much about Russell Street? In the time of the clipper ships, it was lined with bars, flophouses, and brothels. Any time a ship anchored in port, sailors would flood onto the docks and head straight for the night life on Russell. It must've been great! My own bar dates all the way to the turn of the century. It's just about all that's left of those days of glory."

He wandered off again to serve customers, and ended up in a conversation with someone else. I sat alone for quite a while, scribbling in my note pad. Writing is a kind of "trance," for the whole world seems to disappear when I get to putting something down on paper. And because of my special sensitivity, I often find myself "connecting" with things otherworldly as I write. In a moment I had to let my pen lie flat on the paper. I closed my eyes, for I felt *something* that few people would ever detect behind the hum of the day.

"Goin' to sleep on me?"

I was startled back to mundane awareness. Chad had returned, ready to pick up his tale anew. "You know what the most annoying part is? That old boozer Sam keeps snitching my tequila. He drinks nothing else, and lots of it. There's been many a time I'd be in the basement before opening, or after closing hours, and I'd see the tequila delivery bottle start to bubble. That meant someone was up here drawing some of the stuff. This has been happening for going on fourteen years. That's how long I've had the place. I finally learned it never does a lick of good to come running up the back stairs to try to catch who the hell is doing it. It could be Rose, but I think it's Sam. I tried switching the bottles around and I even changed the whole method of delivery. But he always finds the tequila. Doesn't like anything else. Not just a little glass, either; he just sucks it down. I mean, it's a pain in the ass that I have to pay for some dead bastard's binges!"

"You've never seen him materialize?" I asked, which seemed a natural enough conclusion if Chad wasn't sure which ghost was doing the drinking.

"No, but I've heard his voice. Kind of funny sounding. Doesn't make a lot of sense, just some mumbling drunkard who seems ticked off. And now and then, I hear the two shots upstairs—bang! bang! I don't know what it means. Killed Rose, then himself I suppose, but maybe only

Rose. Maybe only himself, but it'd be funny if *that* took two shots."

Joan Irving wandered in, and Chad introduced us. He showed her my card. She didn't laugh, but took it seriously. She could tell I was pretty earnest about ghost-hunting. All the same, I felt a little light-headed, so I said, "What the heck, Chad! Line me up another tomato juice!"

"One for me too, but put something in it." Joan parked herself on the stool next to mine. "So, you're the famous ghost story writer?"

I hadn't heard any mention of my being a writer, only an investigator, so, feeling momentarily important, I asked, "You've heard of me?"

"Nope. Just going by what Chad told me on the phone."

"Oh," I said, the importance knocked out of me. "Chad told me Sam and Rose have been around since the 1960s."

"A lot longer than that, you can well believe! I found Rose's number in an old phone book from the thirties. No one's sure if she was killed or what, but she really did live upstairs, that's for sure. Sam's for real, too. When I ran the place, his room was still padlocked. No one had been in there for decades. There was no key. That's just how spooked people were by the place. But I pried the padlock off and opened up the room. It was all dusty and cobwebby, just like in a scary movie, but I don't get the creeps easy. Sam's bed hadn't been made since he was carried out of there. His wallet was still on the dresser. Had a picture of an old man and an old woman in it, and some loose change, cool old coins. I still have 'em. His long johns were in the middle of the floor. These few things amounted to all his worldly possessions."

Chad put a drink down in front of Joan, then leaned forward to hear the story again.

She said, "I guess I roused him by opening up the place, because after that I often heard him walking back and forth quite a lot. One thing did spook me, though. I'd go up there sometimes, and I'd feel him put his hand on my shoulder. Brrr!"

The evening was getting busier, and the noise level rising. A band was setting up as Joan took me upstairs to see Sam's room. But as we walked by another room, I stopped, feeling a sudden chill up my back. I asked, "Was this Rose's room?"

"No one knows."

"What?"

The band had started playing at a high volume, and the sound through the floor was so loud that I could not hear Joan.

"No one knows!" she said louder.

"I think this was her room!" The music, or the *something*, surrounded me like a glove.

The room was being used for storage. I entered, and immediately the sound of the band downstairs vanished. I looked around and could not see Joan. More surprising still, the boxes that had a moment before been stacked here and there were all gone. Instead, I was standing in a bedroom that seemed recently used. It was a tawdry place, with cheap feminine bric-a-brac everywhere, a dressing table, a gas lamp with a cracked red cover. The bed was a tall four-poster with a badly trumped-up "canopy," which was nothing but an old bedspread tied to the tops of the high posts.

A great many pillows and covers were piled all over the bed, so that at first I didn't realize there were people in that bed. Then I saw the pale, round rear end of a man. Under him was a woman, and she was gazing at me from underneath his bulk. She had a flapper's hairstyle and smeared makeup. I was immediately embarrassed, and was about to apologize for my unexpected intrusion, but in that moment, I realized the woman was not looking at me at all. I doubt she knew I was there. A third party was entering the room and, when the prostitute saw who it was, she looked terrified.

I wanted to turn to see him, but it was as though I were swimming in molasses. My whole body turned slowly, slowly, slowly, until what came into the periphery of my vision was an upraised arm holding a pistol. Two shots rang out. Until then, I had not heard a thing—not the squeaking of the bed, not the intruder's footsteps, nothing. Just those two gunshots. The prostitute's client lurched backward from among piles of covers, then fell to the floor with blood gushing from two holes in his spine.

Rose wept hysterically, but other than the two reports of the pistol, I still could not hear a thing. The room was totally silent. Sam moved to the bedside and threw the gun in Rose's lap. In his left hand he held a huge mug of what I took to be tequila. His right hand, now that it was free of the gun, clutched at his own heart. He staggered out of Rose's room, heading toward his own, where, I suspected, he was momentarily to die of acute alcoholism and heart disease.

The next thing I knew, I was sitting at a table downstairs in the bar. Joan pressed a moist towel to my forehead. The band wasn't playing, doubtless out of curiosity over the woman who had had to be carried down from upstairs. They probably thought I had drunk myself unconscious!

"She's coming 'round," came Chad's familiar voice.

"You're not going to die on us, are you?" asked Joan.

"I'm all right," I said, getting my bearings. "I saw them. Sam killed Rose's client. Then I think he had a heart attack."

"You were out cold up there," Joan told me. "Maybe you were dreaming."

"Maybe you and Chad dreamed about them a bunch of times," I countered.

"Touché," said Chad, laughing.

That evening, relaxing in my room at the bed and breakfast, I finished my notes while everything was still fresh in my mind. Like so many of these hauntings, Jane, nothing ever comes together quite as fully as we'd like. And with ghostly reenactments, I sometimes wonder if the spirits themselves haven't gotten their own histories mixed up! But one thing I felt certain about—though don't ask me to explain why I think this. You see, I don't really believe Sam and Rose knew each other very well. Sam just brooded over her until he couldn't stand it. She barely knew he existed. I'm sure it all came as quite a surprise to her that the drunkard down the hall thought she was worth killing someone over.

I don't know how or when Rose died. I think she lived another ten years, for the things I saw in the room, and her hairstyle as well, were from the twenties. Joan had found evidence that Rose lived there in the thirties. She may never have gotten over what happened, probably wept herself to death, or died of syphilis or poverty after being abandoned by an evil world once her minimal good looks were all used up.

The thing I learn over and over again, Jane, is that the world is full of pain. Yes, it's always been filled with pain, and it always will be. I can only hope that folks like you and me—who investigate the darkest corners of this thing we call reality—I hope we've learned something by what we've seen. If we have, then when Lady Death comes with her final kiss, we'll go with less grief and misery than those who linger.

Love,
Penelope

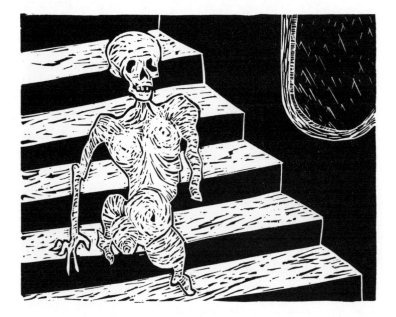

# SARAH,
# THE GHOST OF
# GEORGETOWN CASTLE

*Penelope Pettiweather*
*Seattle, Washington USA*

*Jane Bradshaw*
*Oundle, Northants, England*

My dearest Jane,

**W**hen you encounter ghosts around England, I fancy your having the same range of emotional responses as do I while investigating ghosts of the Great Northwest. You and I live so far apart, and see each other

so rarely, that it is easy to project oneself onto the other—
but I do feel we have a great deal in common. I have
learned again an old lesson about the "one thing" that most
defends us from malevolent darkness, and, as usual, it has to
do with my investigations of occult matters.

In historical Georgetown, there is a big, three-story, turreted
mansion known as the Georgetown Castle, built in 1889. I
phoned one of the two young men who lived there, for I
had long wanted to investigate phenomena associated with
the house. They were friendly fellows, open to my desire
for an interview. I went immediately to Georgetown.

Pat and Jay had been in the house only a few weeks
when they first spied a shadow moving by the closet door.
Pat was very animated when he told me, "Just out of the
corner of my eye I saw something. I looked up, and there
she was!—this old lady looking totally insane! My God, I
tell you—she held one hand around her throat, like this."
He clutched his throat to illustrate. "And with her other
hand she started hitting Jay, like this." He jabbed the air
with his fist to demonstrate.

The ghost, they explained, was a tall, slender, severe-
looking woman with eyes like burning coal, her hair done
up in a Victorian bun, wearing a floor-length white dress.
Floating behind her was a portrait of a swart Mediterranean
man, "whose appearance," said Jay, "had an unavoidable
suggestion of malevolence."

"As I watched the ghost strangling itself and punching Jay," Pat continued, "I was thinking, wait a minute! I'm not crazy! This can't be happening! Then, while she's flailing away at him, Jay all of a sudden says, 'Oh, you must be Sarah,' and just like that she disappeared!"

Jay added, "I've no idea why I called her Sarah. She had somehow informed me this was her name. Have you heard of that before?"

"Yes." I accepted the freshly steeped tea that Jay handed me in a dainty cup. I explained, "Ghosts commonly express incidental telepathy. Or a sensitive viewer's own intuition can be heightened by factors of thousands." Then I asked, "What do you know about the castle's history?"

They explained that for many years before they moved in, the grand old Victorian mansion had been allowed to fall into decay. Neighbors told stories of it having been a bordello and gambling den during the Depression, and that ill-gotten monies were still hidden in the walls. It was a boardinghouse briefly, but failed because no boarder would stay more than a night.

"Once," said Pat, "a Ouija board told previous owners in which wall gold was hidden. They tore out that wall only to have Ouija tell them to tear up another, and then another, until there were holes in all the walls—and that's pretty much the way the place remained until we bought it."

There was, of course, no gold, but only a mischievous Ouija.

Jay continued, "Many people claim to have seen Sarah, for she's not at all shy. She has appeared to our party guests, considerably spicing up our events. She once rummaged through the suitcases of a woman visiting Pat and me from Los Angeles. 'Who was that old lady going through my belongings?' she asked the following morning at breakfast, not having been told about the ghost."

Pat said, "Once I heard a window breaking, but no window was found broken. While investigating, I was assaulted on a staircase, and fled to find Jay, telling him excitedly that something had tried to strangle me. The weird thing is, I didn't think it was Sarah."

"Who, then?" I asked.

"I didn't know who it was—but it must have been a clue as to how she finally died. The sound of the shattered glass was someone breaking into the house one night. I think someone killed the mad old woman believing she had gold hidden about."

"I run a Pioneer Square art gallery," said Jay, "and Sarah took an interest in my work. Whenever I was painting, she'd intrude and start posing. She was insistent in wanting me to do her portrait, perhaps as a mate for the sinister one that sometimes followed her. After I complied with her wish, she was considerably calmer."

"One day," Jay said, "an elderly woman paid us an unannounced visit. She just barged right in and claimed she was the granddaughter of the man who had built the house. She wanted to see what we were doing to the place. Then she noticed the portrait I had done of Sarah, and exclaimed, 'That's my dead great aunt!'"

"She told us the story of Sarah," Pat continued. "In the twenties and thirties, Sarah's brother-in-law had taken over the mansion for his gambling operations and prostitution. His partner, a Spaniard, fell in love with Sarah, and sired a bastard by her. The Spaniard later killed the child and hid the corpse under the porch. He murdered his partner, and reportedly hid a fortune on the premises. Sarah went crazy with anguish for her child and, like her lover, eventually died a violent death."

"Since we learned her story, Sarah has appeared less often," said Jay.

"But," added Pat, "every time we tell someone she's gone, something happens."

"Every time?" I inquired.

"That's right," said Jay, and both of them pointed to Sarah's portrait. Standing beneath it was the old woman herself, no longer strangling herself, but clasping her hands under her throat. Then she turned slowly about and, though seemingly unable to see where I was sitting, she gazed directly at the two young men with tragedy in her features, as though she worried for them constantly. Then she faded from our sight. I let out a long breath.

"She seems to be looking after our well-being," said

Jay. "We've come to be very fond of her, and do wish she wouldn't worry so much."

"Perhaps she has cause to worry," I suggested.

"How so?"

"Your experience on the staircase of being attacked. It's possible the murderous Spaniard lingers as well!"

Pat and Jay turned to one another and winced. I had finished my tea and, thanking them for their courtesies, I left. Those young men are aware that I have a certain skill at convincing unwanted ghosts to leave a place; and I do expect, one day, to be asked to do something about the murderer who follows Sarah in the form of a malevolent portrait. But as for Sarah, she has as much right to live in that house as they. She is, I think, as fortunate as any ghost can be, to have been "adopted" by veritable nephews.

One of the great enemies of evil is love, and for as long as Pat and Jay and Sarah love one another, all darker spirits are harmless. That's a lesson we can all learn.

Love,
Penelope

# FRITZ,
# THE GENTLE GHOST
# OF SHAW ISLAND

*Penelope Pettiweather*
*Seattle, Washington USA*

*Jane Bradshaw*
*Oundle, Northants, England*

Dear Jane,

I am always delighted to receive your letters, and your experience with the kirkyard ghost of that sad child you called Joan was heartwrenching. By a coincidence, late this very morning Mrs. Byrne-Hurliphant dropped by to brag to me of a successful exorcism of an infant ghost. My over-large friend swept into my home with all her layers of over-dress wafting perfume, her stubby arms upraised and her fingers fluttering—I knew instantly that she had come to boast of something or another. And as I listened to her, I found myself filled with sadness for the little spirit and not terribly impressed by my friend's gleeful squashing of its presence. It's bad enough to have died of abuse. But then, from a sorrowful afterlife, "to be done battle," as my witchy friend put it, seems to me all the more wretchedly unnecessary.

The infant she spoke of could be heard weeping on certain holiday nights, but was otherwise detected rarely. It didn't sound to me like any great nuisance. But the new family in the house was very unsettled by it, and so called in the popular witch, who often gets herself in the news with her overblown sensationalism, making all us spirit watchers look like eccentric buffoons. It has always been the philosophy of Mrs. Byrne-Hurliphant that every ghost must be disabused of its habits and squashed as swiftly as possible, no matter how innocuous the spirit seems.

Ordinarily, I might agree that it is best to help any ghost "continue onward" to another plane, where, one can hope, there is greater joy than in lingering. But my witchy friend expresses rather too much exaggerated glee over her successes, and approaches every spirit as though it were hateful. She and I remain friends because of our shared "sensitivity" to things otherworldly, but I must say, her approach is so heartless I sometimes wonder why I tolerate her.

After she left, I found myself pondering ghosts that might well deserve welcome, who add spice to a dwelling, who have as much right as the living to possess a house. I remembered Fritz, the gentle ghost of Shaw Island.

Al and Lotte Wilding's waterfront farmhouse in Blind Bay on Shaw Island, in its pleasant rustic setting, was a comfort not only for the couple, but also for "a gentle little spirit" whom they affectionately called Fritz. When the Wildings put their house and forty acres up for sale in 1987, they cheerfully advertised the existence of the ghost—truly a sales point for the romantically inclined who are not made skittish by invisible housemates.

The Wildings dwelled in the farmhouse for nearly thirty years, though at first it was only a weekend retreat. The ghost was present from the beginning. Lotte said, "You just get used to someone else living there. Once you do that, it's no big deal." They believe the ghost is that of Fritz Lee, who died at the age of twenty-one in the 1918 flu epidemic. He is buried on the property, the equivalent of about a block from the house.

When they first obtained the property, the Wildings found all of Fritz's schoolbooks in his upstairs room, together with letters to his mother. The Wildings had owned the house one year when Al's uncle experienced an unseen presence in that room. At first he tried to dismiss what was happening, but after three uneasy nights, Al's uncle would never sleep in Fritz's room again. It was used for storage throughout the decades to follow.

Fritz's mischief was restricted to poltergeist activity. He never manifested himself visually. Since the house had settled with age, the doors scraped the floors, and did not open easily. Nevertheless, doors would at times open with inexplicable ease when no one was near them.

The Wildings' fond acceptance of the spirit seemed to induce Fritz to spare them any personal nuisance. For the most part, he bothered only guests, who were more easily excited. Al, a retired police officer, once had two fellow officers and their wives at the farmhouse for a weekend. The guests slept in the living room. Awakened by strange footsteps, one of the officers drew his gun. But when the lights were turned on, no one was there. In another incident, a friend of the Wildings' daughter stayed overnight and was certain of a presence at the foot of her bed.

A ghost's taste in music rarely changes from the time of death, and as you know, Jane, many stories are told of ghosts interfering with music they don't like. Fritz was of this kind. Once, when the Wilding children were playing rock and roll on the radio, the station suddenly changed to softer music. They tuned their station back in, only to have the music change a second time. They set the radio on the table and tuned it once more, then sat and watched. The dial didn't move. But the radio soon began to pick up softer music from an earlier era.

Over the years, Fritz behaved aggressively only once. The Wildings' grown daughter, Juliana Barnes, had been staying with them for about two years, but the time came when she prepared to move out. Her leaving upset Fritz. Lotte said, "Juliana and I were alone in the house and I was helping her pack. As I walked down from upstairs—with Juliana in front—I was hit on the back with a pillow. I turned and said, 'It's not my fault she's leaving!' Juliana asked me at the time why I looked so strange. I didn't tell her what had happened until later."

On that same day, pots and pans hanging on hooks swayed and clanged together. Juliana Barnes said, "I thought that was strange. Maybe it's true he didn't want me to leave."

It struck me as quite sad and sweet that even from "the other side," a young ghost could get a painful crush on the living, and regret their parting.

Juliana once told me, "It gives you a strange feeling to have so many of his possessions and know he's buried not far away." She had often felt his presence. Once while Juliana was vacuuming, the unseen Fritz tapped her on the shoulder. "I never felt it was a harmful ghost. Rather than being afraid, I always felt protected by it. It wasn't a mean spirit. But it didn't seem to like strangers."

Her husband, Patrick Barnes, doubted the ghost's

existence. Whenever a wind blew open the yard gate, he'd say, "There goes Fritz!" But twenty-eight years of these phenomena versus his joking skepticism—it's hard to discount the experiences of the whole of the Wilding family.

I must tell you, Jane, that if I heard of Mrs. Byrne-Hurliphant setting out to do away with gentle Fritz, I would be tempted to intervene, to talk the present tenants out of hiring her services. I know how hard it is for some people to tolerate a bit of darkness drifting among them, reminding them of their own mortality. But a little pity just might do us some good, and even the dead want to be loved.

Yours dearly,
Penelope

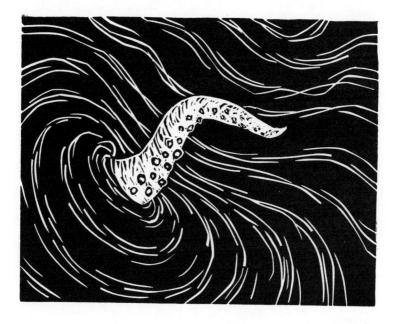

# OGOPOGO

*Penelope Pettiweather*
*Kelowna, British Columbia*

*Jane Bradshaw*
*Oundle, Northants, England*

Dear Jane,

Finally, finally, finally, I have seen Leviathan!

Here I am, lounging in a really very plush "rustic-style" room of a bed and breakfast near eight-mile-long Lake Okanagan in central British Columbia. I'm safe and warm between the sheets, propped against three fat soft pillows. Nevertheless, I am still shaking with excitement, so if my handwriting is a bit unsteady, forgive me. I just had to write to you right away, for I recall telling you in a letter quite some while back that for all the ghosts I have seen in my life, I had somehow never managed to catch sight of a sea serpent or lake monster.

Well, now I have!

It all started as a safe little camping expedition with my pup tent, sleeping bag, and a lantern to read and write by at night. I was staying in a campground. It had running water, showers, a few other niceties, so things weren't exactly primitive. But surrounding this "tamed" woodland area were some of the wildest, most beautiful forests you could imagine.

I walked about all day and was truly overwhelmed by the forest's beauty. Come evening, I retired to my campsite to ruminate and cling to feelings of awe. In the morning, a pleasant, middle-aged ranger named Jack Tobb came around to collect a small fee for the camping space. When he caught my name, wonder of wonders, he knew who I was. Seemed he's quite a reader, and his house was filled with books, including one or two of my own. He came back later in the afternoon and had me sign *Northwest Houses and Their Ghosts*. Then he told everyone else at their campsites—there weren't many, happily enough—that I was a famous author. Far be it for me to correct the exaggeration of "famous"!

This resulted in my being visited throughout the day by various and sundry folks who wanted to share ghost legends and uncanny events. Quite fun that was. By the white-gas light of my lantern, late into my second night, I wrote all of it down before I forgot anything.

I was scribbling away, propped up on my belly with scrap paper rustling under my pen. Then all of a sudden, a grizzled old face poked itself into my pup tent and liked to scare the pee out of me.

It was a years-scarred, stunningly beautiful old Indian woman with braids wrapped around her head. She said, "Twenty dollars, I'll show you N'ha'a'itk. Ten dollars now, ten when you see her."

"Pardon me? You'll show me what?"

"N'ha'a'itk. Mister Jack, he says you would pay me twenty dollars to see N'ha'a'itk."

"Right now? Is it a local ghost?"

"Not a ghost. N'ha'a'itk. White people call her Ogopogo. She's big, but she hides well. Only I can take you. Nobody else can find her for sure. I have a boat. It takes a while to get there. Bring your lantern and something to eat along the way. Ten dollars now."

Well, for ten dollars now and ten later, I wasn't going to pass up the opportunity of night-long adventure with an old Indian woman, whether or not I saw Ogopogo. When she said that name, I knew exactly whom she meant, for Ogopogo is by far the best-known lake monster in the region. I had spoken to several people about that serpent over the years, during various visits to British Columbia, but never before had anyone offered to show the beast to me for twenty dollars.

I turned my lantern on low to save fuel, got into my trousers and shoes, put on a backpack with odds and ends in it—dried fruit, two hastily made sandwiches in case my new friend wanted one, a flashlight, matches, knife, things like that—and gave my guide her "ten dollars now."

"My name's Penelope," I said, as we sauntered through the dark forest by the dim lantern. She wore a long, heavy skirt and hiking boots. She was thin and tall and took such long strides, with such surety in the darkness, I was hard pressed to keep up. Her beautiful face showed great age—I never asked how old, but eighty wouldn't have surprised me—yet she was as spry as I was at twenty.

"I am Mary Beaver-Who-Knows-Something," she replied. "I am the number-one fisherwoman," she added. "That's how I got my name. I know everything that's in this lake."

We came to the shore. There was a small boat half out of the water. In the darkness it looked modern, fiberglass, extremely clean and tidy, with a good deal of fishing gear under the seats and tied to the inner walls. I climbed in and Mary shoved us off. She hopped in and rowed into deeper water, then lowered the motor, and we were off at a steady, slow clip.

"We must go slow," said Mary Beaver-Who-Knows-Something. "There might be logs floating. I know all the logs, but they move."

The moon was bright. I turned off my lantern. The engine was surprisingly quiet, for Mary had it operating slowly. She piloted from the rear, the moonlight full in her upraised face.

"I know a little about Ogopogo," I said. "It was first reported in the 1870s, by a pioneer woman. I think her name was Mrs. John Allison."

"N'ha'a'itk has been here longer than that. My great-grandmother told my grandmother who told my mother who told me where to see her for sure. Women see her more often than men, so I am not surprised a white woman saw her back then. But she was not the first woman to see N'ha'a'itk."

"No, of course not!" I said, a bit embarrassed. "Ogo-pogo—I mean, N'ha'a'itk—she really likes women most? That seems quite curious to me."

"She brings rain and fertility. She blesses women's wombs. She blessed my womb. I have three daughters still alive, and eight granddaughters, and many great-grand-daughters. I am sad to say not many of them care about N'ha'a'itk. One granddaughter cares, and when I am gone, she will be the only one who knows the way to N'ha'a'itk's lair."

"Do you show people at night so they won't know the secret place in the day? Or does N'ha'a'itk only come out after dark?"

"N'ha'a'itk does not prefer the daylight. She doesn't prefer the night. She prefers the time just as the sun gets ready to rise, for she likes the sound of birds. I don't mind if you remember the way to her lair, but it isn't easy for others to tell where it is, even if they have been there before. Still, it is not intentionally my secret. N'ha'a'itk owns this lake, not I. N'ha'a'itk welcomes everyone who honors her."

"I'm greatly interested in the idea she likes women best." I did wonder if the real reason women saw the serpent more than men was that the secret of the lair was held by women, and Mary tended to show the place only to women.

Mary told me the story of one man who had seen N'ha'a'itk. "Long ago, Tayee Timba'skt said, 'Why do only women see N'ha'a'itk? It's because women tell silly stories to each other and to children! There is no N'ha'a'itk!' So he went out in his canoe at dawn. He made a song of disbelief." Mary began to sing Chief Timba'skt's song. "'Nah-ha-ah-ah, nah-ha-ah-ah, there is no N'ha'a'itk, N'ha'a'itk is old women's lies, nah-ha-ah-ah, nah-ha-ah-ah.' But he never sang that song again, because N'ha'a'itk lifted her big tail out of the water and knocked Tayee from his canoe. But N'ha'a'itk never causes trouble to anyone who believes in her power."

I tried to dredge my memory for facts about this lake monster. I remembered that in 1925, the B.C. government actually had a plan to equip ferries on the Okanagan with devices to repel Ogopogo attacks! But they were talked out of it by the half of the people who said there was no Ogopogo, and by the other half who said Ogopogo never hurt anyone. Ferrymen worried, though, because they often bumped against something mysterious—in places where the water was known to be two hundred feet deep!

In 1926, a music hall tune popular in England celebrated Ogopogo, so it would seem she has had an international celebrity. If you ever find the sheet music for it, Jane, I'd appreciate having a copy! The songwriter assumed Ogopogo was male, contrary to Mary Beaver-Who-Knows-Something's belief, and the song went in part,

> I'm looking for Ogopogo
> The bunny-hugging Ogopogo
> His modder wuzza mutton
> His fodder wuzza whale
> I'm gonna put a little bit
> Of salt upon his tail.

Well, Jane, whenever I go traveling about the Northwest, I usually bring a satchel with research materials. So I was able to look at my little file of Okanagan lore after I had checked into this bed and breakfast. I am now able to fill you in on a few things that I could only vaguely recollect as I was sliding through the night atop those black, moonlit waters.

Here, with my notes and newspaper clippings spread around me, I find fishermen in the early 1900s baited huge hooks with slabs of meat, trying to catch Ogopogo. Once there was an attempt to dynamite Ogopogo and make her float to the surface like a dead fish. In 1946, a local orchard farmer shot Ogopogo, and citizen outrage forced the attorney general to issue a document interpreting the Fisheries Act, extending protection to Ogopogo. In essence there is now a special law assuring her continued prosperity.

Over the years, a vast number of people witnessed Ogopogo. Sometimes cars park all along the highway, with gaping onlookers pointing at a fin, a hump of coil, or even the head darting along at the surface of the water. Among those who've gone on record are an Anglican clergyman, two doctors, businessmen from Calgary and Vancouver, an entire construction crew, startled passengers on Greyhound buses, two newspaper publishers…and far more. In July of 1955, Ernest Callas signed a sworn statement, describing a creature with fins along its back, greenish-brown skin of armored texture, four distinct humps, and nearly forty feet in length. Others say it is seventy feet long, and still others that it is only fifteen feet—there may well be a family.

In June of 1976, two men fishing south of Fintry spied the serpent. One told a local paper, "We were three hundred yards off shore. That darned thing was a hundred feet farther out, but the wake was so great it carried us nearly back to land. The creature was blue-black and moved caterpillarlike in the water. Now I know for sure Ogopogo is not a myth."

Roy Patterson McClean, onetime publisher of the *Kelowna Daily Courier*, took his retirement and spent most of his time at his lakefront property. "One day I saw the ducks all stirred up about something. There were hundreds of them flapping about in the water and taking off like the devil was after them. Then I saw three humps parallel to the shore. My first thought was there were three car tires out there. I watched for a minute and a half, then lost sight of them as they went farther out in the lake. I can hardly believe it even now, but there *is* something that lives down there."

The reports are like a litany. In 1949, a Doctor Underhill, with a friend, spotted *two* Ogopogos. Harry and Betty Staines of Westback, in July 1976, saw a thirty-foot black eel easing along at about eight miles an hour. Joe Davignon, a fisherman, saw a snakelike creature of the same length at the north end of the lake. Sam McDonald of Kelowna, another fisherman, said he saw a fifty-foot creature with three humps out of the water, which was momentarily very still, then took off at a high speed. Over the years, there have been several organized Ogopogo hunts. In the summer of 1977, eighty divers working half-hour shifts attempted a complete sweep of the lake, to no avail.

There are several theories about the serpent, none I

would credit. I like the one about a clutch of plesiosaur eggs fast-frozen in the glaciers, then deposited in the lake as the ice melted millions of years later. For myself, if I had to come up with a theory, mine is simply that many animals remain undiscovered by scientists. In fact, every single day another uncatalogued and unnamed creature becomes extinct somewhere in the world—even as you and I, Jane, go about our daily affairs. Some people do worry that Ogopogo will become extinct before real physical evidence of her existence can be established. In the middle-to-late 1970s, Arleen Gaal, a leading Ogopogo authority, organized protests against the use of herbicides in the area, lest the poisons pose a threat to Ogopogo's continued survival.

Mary stopped her boat's engine. It was still very dark as she took up the oars. We were far from the shore, the trees barely visible in outline under stars. Mary said, "N'ha'a'itk doesn't like the motor. I will paddle near her lair. The water is very deep here. You can light your lantern. N'ha'a'itk may want to investigate the light, and you'll get a close look at her."

Not without some slight doubt about getting *too* close a look, I lit the lantern. I took out my flashlight as well. As Mary rowed, I pointed the flashlight into the black waters. In a few more minutes, Mary shipped the oars.

"Should I throw out the anchor?" I asked, indicating a chunk of cement in a large-size coffee can.

"N'ha'a'itk wouldn't like that," said Mary. "The water's too deep anyway. I don't have that much rope."

We waited. For some while there was only the sound of water lapping at the hull and of a distant owl whose voice carried well across the waters. We ate sandwiches and dried fruit, and talked about (of all things!) what would happen after California fell into the sea.

Later, Mary Beaver-Who-Knows-Something began to sing quietly in her elderly but very sweet voice. "Hah-ah-ha-ha, hah-ah-ha-ha, N'ha'a'itk is a pretty maiden, ha-ah, N'ha'a'itk is a strong matron, ha-ah, N'ha'a'itk is an old princess, ishi-nai, ishi-nai, hah-ah, ha-ah."

As she sang, birds on the distant shores joined, providing a lovely countermelody. I noticed that the eastern sky was ever so faintly aglow. Mary's song seemed to be an invitation.

The boat began to rock, not violently, but it was noticeable. I was momentarily alarmed. Mary sat perfectly still, singing her song, which eased my worries. The motion became more pronounced, and the water all around the boat appeared disturbed in some curious manner. There were not exactly waves, but a whirling disruption. I realized the boat was turning around, counterclockwise. This continued as the sky lightened from darkest indigo, becoming paler and paler by the minute.

Around and around the boat turned slowly, slowly, until finally the disruption from below stopped and the boat eased itself still.

Mary stopped her song. I looked her right in the face and saw such serenity there that I, too, felt only serenity. The shoreline's bird population now gave a great chorus indeed. I was absorbed in that sound, expecting nothing more of my adventure, needing nothing more to count it a success.

I had been awake the whole night, but felt more relaxed than drowsy. When I was most at peace, one serpentine loop and then another and then another arose from the lake. The creature was less than thirty feet off the bow, and appeared to be twenty or thirty feet long even with most of itself submerged. A fourth loop rose and I'd just about decided that the tail must be only ten feet away from the boat, just under the surface of the water.

Wrong. The *head* was nearest the boat. N'ha'a'itk raised her face straight up out of the water! She gazed at the vulnerable little boat or at my lantern.

N'ha'a'itk had a distinctly *mammalian* face—somewhere between a seal and baby lamb, but far bigger and broader. The dark, moist eyes were now focused entirely upon me, as mine were upon her. The lamplight went out —it was out of gas—and still the gleam remained in N'ha'a'itk's eyes. There was *wisdom* in those eyes, though I'm sure I only project my interpretation.

Less than three minutes passed, but it felt like hours. The sun rose, and N'ha'a'itk sank back into the water.

Mary and I sat quietly for a long time. We communed with the wholeness of the earth. Something mystically important had happened.

I think Mary understood how impressed I was, how glad I was that she had invited me to this place, how I never would forget this night or her singing with the birds or the rising sun or the visit from N'ha'a'itk. She smiled at me with grandmotherly tenderness.

Then she put an open hand toward me and, with extraordinary sweetness, said, "Ten dollars please."

Love,
Penelope

# THE
# QUEEN
# MUM

*Anna Christopherine Bailey*
*Portland, Oregon*

*Penelope Pettiweather*
*Seattle, Washington*

Dear Penelope,

I bet you're surprised to hear from me after so long. I'm a "Bailey" now, not a "Berman." Many of my old interests have fallen by the way—with only a twinge of regret.

You must understand, Penny, that not all of us with "the extra sense" have the stamina to always be investigating things. I married, gave birth to a handsome little brat, and my husband disapproves of "the ghostie habit," as you once called it in a letter to me. So bit by bit, I faded from the inner circle of mystical delights.

Small things do still happen of course—it can't be stopped—but I no longer go out of my way to experience the unknown. You'll say it's a great pity, a waste of talent. As for myself, I came to the conclusion long ago that two kinds of talents just don't matter for a darn in our time. One is ghost-hunting. The other is writing poetry. No loss that I've given up both.

But something wholly unexpected happened to me recently. My husband (otherwise a dear fellow) doesn't want to hear such news. So I thought I had just better drop you a few lines while the brat is napping and the Master is away.

I don't know how to tell it really. It began so innocuously. As you know, we live practically in the inner city. I can walk to the Hawthorne district and do all my shopping. I don't have to learn to drive, yet I don't have to feel isolated for not driving. I love this area; it's gotten increasingly eccentric. Bookstores, coffeehouses, cafés, useless shops that sell chipped or worn-out gewgaws they call antiques, and a pet shop with lizards. What else could anyone desire? If not for my baby carriage, I could almost imagine myself a Bohemian once again. I know I've come to live too darned normal a life, but I do still like to be surrounded by all these artists and queer folks. Otherwise, I'd feel like a ghost myself.

The downside is a growing share of homeless who apparently agree it's quite a nice neighborhood. I get to feeling so dreadfully guilty about my life, first for becoming a commonplace bean head, and secondly for being pretty comfortable. A lot of people out there aren't comfortable at all. I've allowed myself to become a "soft touch," especially with the homeless women. They're so *dirty*, and waste funds on cigarettes—yet I feel more anguish than annoyance when they panhandle me.

By now they "see me coming a mile away," so to speak, as I've taken to buying whole rolls of coins to keep with me when I go to Hawthorne. I don't pride myself on it; I just haven't the foggiest notion what else to do beyond saying "yes" when asked for coins.

I do at least gain a few pointless adventures from my low-budget acts of charity. Once, at a month's end, when Jeff's paycheck hadn't lasted quite long enough, I simply didn't have any change for anyone. I felt so apologetic to the "regulars" that I inanely took a tampon out of my purse and gave *that* to a young homeless woman. You wouldn't believe how excited she got! It never before occurred to me how difficult it must be to get tampons if you live on the streets. Now she never asks me for change at all—just tampons!

But let me tell you, there is this one old lady, and I mean *old*; she's like something out of a horror movie. Oh, I know you, Penny, you're going to say I'm an ageist, that old people are good-looking too, but jeez, there are limits. Imagine if you can the oldest woman you've ever seen, and not one who has aged very gracefully either. Now add about a thousand extra wrinkles and big folds of skin sagging off her face, jowls like two stained paper sacks crinkled up and glued on her cheeks, and hair as thin and mangy as a flea-infested rat's. Add, as well, two big red cups under her eyes. I don't know what else to call them. Her lower eyelids have somehow turned down, becoming enormous cups that always ooze thick, yellowish tears. It's disgusting. And when she holds her hand out to me for quarters, it's like a stick off an old dead tree being poked at you.

She wears big black shoes and layer upon layer of the most fantastic clothing—not just old clothes, but *old* clothes, like she steals them from vintage shops. They're not all that dirty, either, though certainly they haven't been ironed in a couple of decades.

To top this off, she wears a banged-up old tiara with some of the glass "diamonds" popped out. She says it's her crown, and fancies herself the queen mother of Oregon!

She takes good care of herself, I give her that. She smells like powder and cheap perfume, with just a tinge of decay—awful enough, but nothing compared to the other beggars. At first I assumed she did have a home somewhere, or she wouldn't have been able to keep herself so neat. I guessed she begged mainly because it's hard to make ends meet on social security, but at the end of a day, she had a reasonable place to sleep.

But after talking to her several times, I caught on that she really was homeless. She says, "I used to have a nice house in Hillsboro, but I don't now."

The other street people honored her claim to being queen mother of Oregon, and called her Queen Mum or Queen Mary. She told me her name was Mary Woods, and she was from Knoxville, Tennessee, but had lived in Oregon a good long while. At times, she has this delusion that George Washington is still president. When corrected, he becomes President Taft.

I was out with the brat, pushing his carriage along Hawthorne, when Queen Mum shambled out from a dark doorstep and got in the way. She bent down to play with Jeff Junior, poking him with those five skinny sticks that pass for fingers. She ichy-cooed and wuzzy-wuzzied until Jeff managed to get his little, stubby, candy-stickied fingers in her hair to make a grab for the tiara. It was so knotted into her hair, Jeffy couldn't possibly get it off, but he sure made her howl.

That's when Queen Mum got wild. She clutched at her banged-up old tiara and staggered away, trying to shout. She couldn't shout very well, but she made a pretty ugly noise trying. She told passersby that my son had tried to usurp her, that he was a pretender to the throne, but she had been duly made queen in 1908, and would never abdicate. Hers was a position for life, and no one would ever succeed in murdering her and taking away her crown.

Whew. I guess that tiara's the only important thing she has left, but knowing that didn't make it easier for me. It was exceedingly embarrassing. I tried to leave, but she followed me, insistently complaining about my son's attempt to overthrow the queen. "Your little sonny will never be king! He can't kill me! They tried to bury me before, but I got up! I'm the queen mother of Oregon, always will be! I'm older than the constitution of the state! I *am* Oregon! Oregon is *me!* If you shoot me, sonny, you shoot the very earth you stand on! You'll fall in the black pit you shot in the ground, and you won't get out. That's what you'll do, but you'll never get the crown!"

Her tirade went on for quite some while, and was a lot more colorful than I can relate. She tossed her hands around like some kind of mad puppet, and her hair stood straight out on all sides. Jeez, I hated it. I hated ever having given any one of those damned beggars a single quarter if all it got me was being chased back home by the ugliest old hag I'd ever seen in my life. It put me in a black, black mood, and as a result, I was too frightened to go anywhere for two weeks after, for fear she'd chase me again.

I had nightmares about her, too. In the longest one,

she was in a big auditorium, together with the mayor, black-frocked ministers, businessmen, society matrons— the leading lights of the city, with their families, all of them dressed to the nines. They were making a great to-do over Queen Mum. She was slightly less ugly in my dream than in real life, but that's not saying much. The whole affair looked like a lot of fun, but something in the *mood* made it a nightmare. Every laughing face appeared to have a spider hiding under the tongue. Every shuffle of foot was accompanied by the rattle of dice inside their shoes. And the dream had a *stink* of mustiness and mothballs and Queen Mum's horrible perfume.

I was in a complete dither over her. I had fantasies of murdering her so that I could walk on Hawthorne and not feel threatened. But when I finally got myself up and out of my blues and worked up the nerve to do some needed shopping, I saw her again. She didn't act especially strange (for her, at least). I don't think she remembered a thing about the event that had haunted me for the last two weeks. She stuck her hideous mummy hand at me. I gave her a quarter and she toddled off muttering the blessings of the queen.

Now I must jump to the end, because only last week I was in the downtown library looking at old newspapers. If you must know why, it was for Jeff Senior. His birthday is soon, and I have been secretly creating a book with calligraphy, which lists everything that happened in Oregon on his birthday for a hundred years.

One occurrence on Jeff's birthday was a coronation. I sat gazing at the microfilm screen, reading this old article dated 1908, and I could hardly believe the coincidences. It said, among other things I'll leave out:

> Mrs. Mary Ramsey Lemons Woods of Knoxville, Tennessee, came to Oregon in 1853, and lives in Hillsboro. She was two years old when George Washington became President. This year, she turned one hundred twenty years old. For the oldest woman in Oregon, there was a celebration at Portland's Marquam Theater last night, and Mrs. Woods was duly crowned queen mother of the state of Oregon.

And, I suppose, a good time was had by all.

There's one last thing I want to leave you with, Penny, and then I'll close. Despite some recurring sadness about living this ordinary life, as an ordinary mother of an ordinary child, with a more-than-ordinary husband, I really feel that this existence provides me with a lifesaving raft in a turbulent world. I find myself drawn more and more intensely to Queen Mum. I give her offerings of sweet rolls as though she were a divinity. I buy her lunches and Jeff Junior is learning to say "Queen Mum" when he can't yet say daddy. And I know, I just know, that the reason I feel such empathy for these homeless people is not out of any social concern, but because I'm too damned aware that not very far inside me, I'm a crazy bugger who will be a homeless beggar if I'm not careful. And I truly believe there walks this earth a woman born in the 1700s who is very close, now, to seeing the twenty-first century.

Your puzzled friend,
Anna-Chrissy

# JEREMIAH

*Je suis dégoûté de tout.*
—René Crevel, 1935

My dear Jane,

I 'm glad you received that copy of *Satan's Circus* by Lady
Eleanor Smith. One frets about the overseas mail. You'll
note that while the spine says the publisher is "Doran," the
title page says "Bobbs Merrill," yet it purports to be the first
edition. I'm told that Doran had a habit, in those days, of
purchasing unbound sheets of other publishers' overruns
and reissuing them under the Doran imprint. So you see,
it isn't really the first edition except on the inside! I was also
delighted by your perceptive comments on the outstanding

story "Wittington's Cat." The compiler of *Giddy's Ghost Story Guide* completely misunderstood that one, didn't he?

Thank you for that perfect copy of *Stone-ground Ghost Stories*. I could never have afforded it over here. You'd pale at the American prices for old British books! The stories struck me as quaintly amusing rather than horrific, but there is a lot more to them than meets the eye, though once more, the compiler of *Giddy's* failed to see much in them. There's so much to the central protagonist's character that could be further explored if some talented and enterprising fellow ever wished to add new episodes about the haunted vicar and his parish.

But, enough of mere fictional ghosts. I was chilled to the bone by your recent experience with those two paintings, "Gravedigger" and "Death," you were restoring. If you wrote that one up as a "fictional" adventure, you could certainly sell it to one of the fantasy magazines. They needn't know it actually happened. But what a shame the pictures ultimately had to be covered up. Not that I blame you; still, I'd like to have seen the one of Death on my next trip abroad, and that won't be possible now that it's safely "preserved" under whitewash.

Did my colleague Mrs. Byrne-Hurliphant bother you *that* much on her English journey? She can be a pest, certainly. Please forgive my giving her your address. Now, at least, you'll know exactly what I'm on about!

Yes, yes, I did promise to tell you what happened over

Christmas if you'd tell me that horrid adventure with the paintings. Well, a bargain is a bargain, so now I suppose I must. It's more terrible than any of the little accounts I've sent to Cyril for his antiquarian journal. So brace yourself, and remember—you asked.

It was three weeks to Christmas. I planned holidays alone. All my friends would be off to other states to visit kin. And while Christmas is no big thing to me—growing up with both Eastern European Jews and Southeast Asian Buddhists in one's motley family helps to weaken the impact of Christian holidays—it can yet be gloomy and sad when one's options are unexpectedly restricted. I can't count a couple of pre-Christmas parties I would probably attend. The fact that people are so fantastically tedious makes the *doing* something as depressing as the *not,* so you can see I was in no mood for anything.

I'd finished some early grocery shopping and was coming up the back stairs out of a bleak afternoon rain, two bags squashed in my arms, when I heard the phone ringing. You just know when you hurry, things take longer. I dropped the keys. Then I tried the wrong key. Then I tried the right key upside down. By the time I'd tossed the torn bags and their contents across the kitchen table and grabbed the receiver, all I heard was a faint "click." Surprising how discouraging that click can be at times.

But before I'd put all the groceries away, and pulled

together the majority of the bulk beans I'd scattered, the phone rang again.

It was the feeblest voice I had ever heard.

"Miss Pettiweather?"

"Absolutely," I replied, affecting the prim and the resolute.

"I beg your pardon?" said the faint, elderly voice of a woman who must have been a hundred and fifty-eight if her age matched such a sad, rasping, tired timbre.

"Yes, this is Miss Pettiweather," I said, donning a more conservative aspect.

"I read your article in *The Seattle Times*," said the cracked old voice. "The one about the haunted houses."

I winced. It hadn't been an article but an interview. And while the reporter tried her best to be straight-faced, the writing was so garbled and misquoted that even I had to wonder if the interviewee weren't a lunatic.

"Did you?" I asked affably.

The feeble voice said, "If it happens to me again, I don't think I can make it."

It seemed she was on the verge of tears.

"What's happened?" I was worried this wretched woman was truly in need of my special talents, but so old it would be difficult for her to communicate her problem. "Who am I speaking to?"

"Gretta Adamson," she said. "My heart isn't as good as it was. If he does it again, I'll die. I tried to tell the doctor, but he said not to excite myself. He doesn't believe me. Do you believe me, Miss Pettiweather? Won't anyone believe me?"

"Oh, I can believe just about anything; but I don't know a thing about it as yet, miss—missus?"

"I'm widowed."

"Mrs. Adamson. You haven't told me…"

"It's Jeremiah," she said. "He comes back."

"Is it bad?" I asked. That was the simplest way I could put the question. And she answered even more simply.

"It's terrible."

Then very quietly, very sadly, she added: "Every Christmas. But…but…" She broke down at that point and could barely finish. "He isn't the same."

She lived alone in a small, rundown home in a rundown part of the city. The house hadn't been painted in a full generation, for even curls and flakes had long since come loose and disappeared, so that the whole gray structure looked as though it had never been painted at all. Most of the windows were cracked; some of the cracks were taped; a few small panes had been replaced with wood or plastic.

The lawn was a miniature meadow for inner-city field mice. A wooden fence set her small property apart from the surrounding houses and cheap low-rise apartment buildings. The fence was falling down in places. The front gate was held closed with a length of rope, which had been

woven about in a curious manner, as though the inhabitant
beyond had a secret method no one else could duplicate,
thereby making it possible to tell whenever someone had
tinkered with it. I retied the gate in a much simpler manner, then strode a broken-stone walkway between the two
halves of her little meadow of frozen, brittle grass.

When Mrs. Adamson opened the door, her white,
creased face looked up at me from so far down, it made me
feel like a giant. In her gaze was a world of pitiful hope,
worry, and despair. Her head was cocked completely on
its side, resting on a shoulder in a spectacularly unnatural
posture.

"I'm Miss Pettiweather," I said, hoping my ordinary
demeanor and harmless, frumpy middle age would be
enough to reassure her. In such a neighborhood, it was no
wonder she was leery of opening her own front door.

She was badly hunchbacked and the spinal deteriora-
tion caused her obvious pain. The smell of medicine assured me she had a doctor's care at least. Her neck was so
badly twisted that her left ear was pressed against her shoulder and she could by no method straighten her head. But
a kind soul was inside that ruined body, and kind eyes gazed
up at me.

I followed her into the dimly lit, grubby interior. Her
shuffling gait was slow and awkward, since it was difficult
to walk with such a horribly calcium-leached spine. For her
own part, she seemed to count herself lucky to be able to

walk, and bore up boldly.

She was eighty-five.

"Jeremiah died when I was seventy," she said in her familiar, cracked voice. I sat with her at her kitchen table. "Fifteen years ago, Christmas Eve, in Swedish Hospital."

"What did he die of?" I asked, moving my rickety chair closer to Mrs. Adamson, to better hear her thin, distant voice.

"He was old."

"Yes, I know, but, well, it'll help me to know more. Was he in his right mind? I'm sorry to be so blunt, Mrs. Adamson, but it's only a few days to Christmas. I assure you I *can* help, but I'll need as much information beforehand as you can give me. Was he able to think clearly until close to the end?"

"Lord, no," she said, her sideways head staring with the brightest, sharpest, bluest eyes. "He had Alzheimer's."

I sighed. I would have to grill her a bit more to find out what Mr. Adamson's final days were like. But I could already guess and later, after an interview at Swedish Hospital, I would be certain. The raving last moments, the delusions—in this case, the delusion he had gotten into such a state because his wife had poisoned him. Often, more malignant spirits died in abject confusion, anger, and horror, hence they could not go on to a better existence elsewhere.

The kettle whistled and though I insisted I could make

tea myself, Mrs. Adamson obviously wished to entertain me. She got up, for all the agony of motion, and toddled weirdly around the vile kitchen. A moldy pork chop sat in hard grease in a rusty pan on the stove. A garbage bag was filled with tuna fish and Chef Boyardee spaghetti cans. Something totally beyond recognition reposed on a plate upon the counter, and though the food was days old, whatever it was appeared to have been nibbled on that very morning, whether by Mrs. Adamson or some rat, I didn't want to speculate.

In some ways she was as sharp as could be. In others, she was indubitably senile. I kept her company through the long afternoon. She rambled on about all kinds of things, mostly pretty dull, but was so terribly lonesome I couldn't allow myself to leave. Fifteen years a widow! And each year she had spent Christmas alone in that crumbling house, every year awaiting—Jeremiah. The toughness of someone that frail was really surprising, though such stoicism had left its mark.

She was cheered no end that I promised to spend Christmas Eve with her. I think her relief wasn't entirely because I convinced her I could lay Jeremiah to rest. Fifteen years is also a lot of Christmases spent alone. Such loneliness is hard to bear, even had there not been the terror of a ghost. So it seemed as though Mrs. Adamson was more interested in our Christmas Eve together than in the laying of a ghost. Indeed, she took for granted I could save her from the long-endured horror, and was more worried about the months or years she might have yet to live by whatever means available.

Later that evening, at home in my own warm bed, I was filled with sorrow to think of her. I fought back tears as I pondered that wreck of a body, the years of desperation, the terrible thing she faced year in and year out, darkening her whole life. What will *our* last years be like, Jane? Who will come to visit us? Who will keep us company when we've lost even the skill to write our letters?

I was so involved with her pitiable material situation, I was not preparing myself sufficiently for my encounter with Jeremiah. What could be worse than a sick old age, separated from the rest of the world? Well, Jane, something *can* be worse, as you and I have learned and relearned in our explorations. But I wasn't thinking so on the day I met old Gretta Adamson.

Her odd, sad sort of strength was the other thing that left me unprepared, and the simple way she took for granted that I would put an end to the horrors. She had looked so frail and had endured so long, how could I have expected her particular demon to be a bad one? I wasn't ready, that's all. Though I did my research, I never imagined surprises were waiting.

I visited Mrs. Adamson on two other occasions before the holiday to reassure her about my research at the hospital where her husband died. She hadn't known the worst of his last hours, as she had been ill herself, and unable to be constantly at his side. The day he died, she had been with him only a short time in the morning, thus was spared the worst of his venomous accusations, hallucinations, and the screaming hatred that was a prelude to his death rattle.

I had talked to a head nurse who had been a night nurse at the beginning of her career fifteen years before; she gave me a vivid, startling account of Jeremiah Adamson's raging thirst for revenge against a wife he imagined to be his murderess. I certainly wasn't going to fill in Mrs. Adamson at this late date, and was therefore careful to avoid telling her too much of what I had discovered.

That the head nurse remembered so much should have been a warning to me, as death is too common in hospitals for a nurse to recall one old man in detail. But I chalked it up to her youthfulness at the time—we all remember our first encounters with grotesque tragedy—and Jeremiah *had* been memorably inventive in his repellent promises, given his otherwise impaired faculties.

So I had learned all too well Jeremiah's state of mind in his last moments of senile dementia. Mrs. Adamson was able to tell me a bit more, and remembered other things piece by piece whenever I probed as gently as the situation allowed. But I couldn't delve far at a time, for some of it was too much for her to bear recalling. Much else, I presumed, was genuinely lost to her own age-related difficulties with memory.

"I would like to see Jeremiah's personal papers, what-ever you may have," I said a couple of days before Christ-mas Eve. Mrs. Adamson was aghast, for she herself had never interfered with his privacy, had never sorted through his personal letters and whatnots in the fifteen years since his death. This should have been another clue informing me that Jeremiah's tyranny had begun well before senility set in. But I continued to be blind. I thought only to con-vince Mrs. Adamson of what was essential.

"You see," I explained, "I have to find out more about him. You mustn't think of the ghost as really being Jeremiah. It's only a shadow of him, and a shadow of his darkest mood at that. The afterlife mentality is very simple compared to life. It fixes on a few things. In his private pa-pers, there may be some clue to the thing he most feared or most wanted, and whatever it is can become a tool to erase his lingering shade."

"He wouldn't like us to know those things," Mrs. Adamson insisted, protecting her husband with a peculiar devotion, and looking at me sadly with those sharp blue eyes in her sideways expression.

"Do you know the meaning of an exorcism, Mrs. Adamson?" She wasn't Catholic and wouldn't know much, but of course everyone knows a little. "There are many ways to lay a ghost, but exorcism is the cruelest. It is a real fight. It's terrible for the exorcist and for the ghost. But there are other means. Sometimes you can reason with them, but it's like reasoning with a child. You have to be careful. But think a minute, Mrs. Adamson, about the classic type of exorcism you may have heard about, with holy water and the cross of Jesus. To tell the truth, such a procedure is worthless unless the individual had some personal belief in these things while living. The cross of Jesus is a powerful amulet against the ghost of a Catholic. But if he wasn't mindful of holy things in life, then his ghost won't care about them either.

"Other items can become equally significant. Once I got rid of a ghost by showing it a rare postage stamp it had never been able to get when living. A pretty rotten spirit it was, too, but gentle as a lamb when it saw that stamp. And the ghost never showed up again.

"Only by careful research can I find out what that special item might be. The more personal the papers, Mrs. Adamson, the better."

She sat like a collapsed rag doll in her big, overstuffed chair, pondering all that I had told her, her bright eyes expressing what a dreadful decision I was forcing her to make. At length I helped her stand, reassuring her the whole while, and she led me to a musty closet where we were able to dig out two shoe boxes held together with rubber bands so old they had melted into the cardboard.

Inside were faded photographs and mementos and yellowed letters and a lock of baby's hair in a red envelope labeled "Jeremiah."

"I recollect that," said Mrs. Adamson. "Jeremiah showed it to me. He had a lot of hair when he was a baby. Lost it all."

And her dry, horrible, old voice managed a sweet laugh as she fumbled the envelope open and gazed at the little curl of hair tied with a piece of thread.

She told me, as best she could, who the people were in the family photos.

She became silent on discovering, for the first time in her whole long life, that Jeremiah had once been unfaithful, the evidence being a love letter written by her rival several years *after* Jeremiah married Gretta.

I patted her liver-spotted hand and assured her, "It's sometimes just this sort of thing that brings them back. He may have wanted to spare you knowing."

But that kind of haunting was rarely menacing, so I kept sorting through the two boxes. Jeremiah had kept no diaries—usually women do that, and they're the most easily laid as a result—and there didn't seem to be many clues to what it would take to lay Jeremiah come Christmas Eve.

In the bottom of the second box, I found an old black-and-white photograph of the handsome young man and the strikingly good-looking woman I'd learned were Jeremiah and Gretta when they were courting. What a smile he had! He wore a soldier's bloomers. Her hair was short and little curls hung out from under a flowered hat. Very modern, both of them, in their day. As I looked at this image a long time, the bent, old woman beside me leaned to one side to see what I was studying. She went misty-eyed at once.

In the photo, Gretta was holding a round Japanese fan. The camera had focused well enough that I could make out a floral design painted on it.

"Jeremiah gave me that fan," she said. "I still have it."

And she rose painfully from the chair beside me and tottered into her bedroom. She returned with the antique fan, dusty and faded from having been displayed in count- less ways over countless years. To see that crooked old lady holding that fan, and to see the young beauty holding it in the picture in my hands, well, I cannot tell you how I felt. And she was so moony and oddly happy in her expression, I was once again convinced Jeremiah's ghost couldn't be all that bad, or she wouldn't still think of him tenderly.

"That picture was taken the day we were engaged. He'd been to fight in Asia, and for all we knew might fight somewhere else soon and die. He gave me this fan and I've always kept it."

"It's our cross of Jesus," I said, somehow overawed by the loving emanations from the woman as she held that fan.

"Do you think so?" she asked.

"Jeremiah died with the delusion that you wanted to hurt him, Gretta." I told her this as gently as possible. "That fan will remind him that such a delusion couldn't have been true."

I'd been helping people get rid of ghosts a long time, Jane. I really thought I had it worked out.

On Christmas Eve, I came to Gretta's house early and brought a chicken casserole and a small gift. She was overwhelmed and wept for joy. And we did not mention Jeremiah during our humble repast, for it would have put a pall on our cross-generational friendship and Gretta's first holiday with anyone in many a long year.

She tittered pleasantly and made her usual horrible tea in dirty cups. The Christmas spirit was so much upon me that I actually drank the terrible stuff without worrying if it was infested with beetles. She opened the smartly wrapped present—nothing special, just an old Chinese snuff bottle that I'd had for years and been quite fond of. It had roses carved on two sides and seemed appropriate, because we'd talked about roses a few days earlier.

Then to my surprise, Gretta came up with a box as well—wrapped in quaint, faded, crinkled paper recycled from two decades before, and crookedly taped all over with yellowing, gooey, transparent tape.

In the box was a tiny ceramic doll that must have been fifty or sixty years old if it was a day, and far more valuable than the bottle I'd wrapped for Gretta. I raved about the beauty of the tiny doll, coddled it tenderly, and really didn't have to put on an act. I was honestly overwhelmed.

"It was my grandmother's," said Gretta, at which my

jaw dropped open, realizing my guess of fifty or sixty years was off by a full century.

"You shouldn't part with it!" I exclaimed. "It must be terribly valuable."

"I won't need it any longer, Penelope. In fact, I haven't needed it for years. I almost couldn't find it for you. So you be pleased to take it and don't go thinking it's too much."

Our eyes held one another a long while. How ashamed I was of what I had thought of that bent-necked, hunchbacked woman when first I laid eyes on her. Not that I ever thought ill. But it wasn't her humanity that struck me at the start. I had first noticed her crippled body, her loneliness, her wretched old age, and the decades of accumulating dirt and clutter that surrounded her fading existence. Somewhere down the list of my early impressions, I must have noted her own unique individuality, but it hadn't been the first thing.

And now, despite that she looked at me with her head fused to one side, her face turned up from her permanently crooked posture, I could see—how clearly I could see—that *this* was indeed the young beauty of that old photograph.

We sang carols out of tune and reminisced about our childhood winters; we laughed and we bawled and had a grand day together. She remembered her youth with far greater clarity than she could recall her widowed years. Then about nine-thirty, she was terribly worn out. Though she ordinarily didn't require much sleep, this had been quite an exciting day. She could barely keep her eyes open.

"Gretta," I said, "we've got to put you to bed. No, don't argue. If you're thinking of waiting up for Jeremiah, there's no need. I've got your fan right here, and with it I will lay him flat; you won't even be disturbed. When you wake in the morning, I'll be there on your sofa, and we'll celebrate a peaceful Christmas day."

It was a half-hour more before I actually got her to bed, somewhat after ten. Though she insisted she would be wide awake if I needed her at midnight, she was snoring in homely fashion even before I closed her bedroom door.

I walked down the hall, passed the kitchen, and entered the dining room. I surveyed the room and began quietly to push Gretta's furniture against one wall. She had told me in one of our earlier interviews that Jeremiah would first appear at the living room window and make his way to the kitchen and thence to her bedroom. I went into the living room to move that furniture out of the way also. Such precautions were probably excessive, but I didn't want to stumble into anything if for some unforeseen reason I had to move quickly.

It was still some while to midnight, so I turned on Gretta's radio very quietly and listened to a program about change-ringing. The day had been tiring for me as well. Like Gretta, I thought I would be wide awake until midnight. But the next thing I knew, the radio station was signing off the air, and I was startled awake by a change in the house's atmosphere.

I was not immediately alert. The realization that it was suddenly midnight, coupled with a vague movement beyond the front room window, caused me to stand abruptly from where I'd napped. The sudden motion made my head swim. A black cloud swirled around me. The brittle paper fan had fallen from my lap onto the floor. I bent to pick it up and nearly lost consciousness. I forced my mind to be more fully awake, slowly realizing my dizziness wasn't the natural cause of standing too quickly, but was imposed upon me by something *other*.

As I picked up the fan and moved toward the window, I was brought up short by Jeremiah's sudden appearance there. His black gums were bared, revealing a lack of teeth and reminding me of a lamprey. His eyes were fogged white, as though he were able to see only what he imagined and not what was. It was a complete materialization and he might easily have been taken for a mad Peeping Tom. He raised both his hands, which were bony claws, and shoved them writhing toward the glass. I expected it to shatter, but instead, the specter vanished.

By the increasing chill, I knew he was in the house.

I hurried toward the kitchen, recovering my senses more than not, holding the paper fan before me. I was shaking frightfully, beginning to comprehend the depth of his malignancy.

He was in the kitchen, bent down, scrabbling wildly but noiselessly at the door under the sink. The cupboard opened under his insistence, and he tried to grasp a little faded blue carton, but his clawed hands only passed through it.

Then he stiffened and slowly stood, his back to me. He sensed my presence, and his very awareness gave me shivers. His shoulders stiffened. He began slowly to turn. I took a strong posture and held the paper fan in front of me, so that it would be the first thing he saw.

He turned and, for a moment, was no longer a spidery old man. He was a young soldier, and he looked at me with sharp but unseeing eyes. I can only describe it thus because, although his gaze fell directly on me and was no longer clouded white, he seemed to see something infinitely more pleasing to him than I could have been. I supposed he thought I was Gretta, and he was imposing upon my form his memory of her when she was as young as he himself now appeared to be.

He came forward with such a look of love and devotion that in spite of my persisting alarm, and due I'm sure to some occult influence rather than my own nature, I was momentarily terribly aroused. He reached outward to clasp his youthful hands at the sides of my shoulders. I held my ground, certain that my humane exorcism was having its intended effect.

When his ghostly fingers touched me, I felt a warming vibration, as though my whole upper body were encased in fine electrical wire, the voltage slowly increasing. The fan began to shine so brightly that I felt I risked blindness if I failed to close my eyes, but close them I could not.

Before my gaze, the young Jeremiah's angelic face grew sinister rapidly. Simultaneously, the electricity that held me in anguished thrall became more painful. His perfect smile became twisted; his white teeth yellowed and grew long as his gums receded, and then there was only that toothless maw yelling at me without making a sound, dreadful threats I blessedly could not hear. The young soldier had withered and wizened; it was evil rather than years that aged him. The claws that gripped my shoulders drew blood.

When he let go, the light of the fan went out, and I collapsed to the floor, half sitting against the door jamb. Jeremiah loomed over me with menace, yet my rattled thoughts were pondering in a distant, withdrawn place. I wondered idly if the electrical shock had stopped my heart. I was dimly aware that my lips were wet with froth and drool, and for a moment I was concerned mainly with the nuisance of being unable to move my arm to wipe my mouth.

If these things were the usual result of my investigations, I should not be so in love with haunted places. I have occasionally felt real danger, but this was the first time I had been so insufficiently prepared that physical harm became inevitable.

His blackening claw grasped me anew and he dragged me across the kitchen floor. His other hand wound into my hair as he pushed my face under the sink, so that I saw before my eyes a thirty- or forty-year-old package of poison —from the days when it was still possible to purchase strychnine to kill rats or even wolves—a damp-stained blue package with skull and crossbones printed in black.

And I realized at that moment what I had overlooked: the critical information without which I was helpless before so malignant a spirit. *Gretta had indeed poisoned her husband*, out of love I do not doubt, to end his awful suffering. It explained why, on that Christmas Eve fifteen years before, she had spent only a few minutes with him. There would have been no reason for the physicians to suspect such a thing. But Jeremiah had known, though he lacked the capacity to understand it as an act of mercy.

And now my face was shoved hard against the open package of poisonous salts. I clamped my eyes and mouth shut. Jeremiah's ghost was trying to kill me, and at that moment I felt he had a good chance at success.

Then a sad, raspy voice came from the kitchen doorway, saying, "Let her go, Jeremiah. It's me you want."

The calm resignation in her voice was heartbreaking.

The black claws let go of my arm and hair. I pushed myself away from under the sink. I was still smarting from the shock of Jeremiah's first touch. I could barely see, and when I tried to focus, it looked as though a young woman were moving toward me in a dressing gown. She reached across my shoulder and removed the strychnine from under the sink. A sweet, youthful voice said, "I guess I should have told you all of it, Penelope, but I thought you could stop him from coming without knowing everything. I'm sorry. Now it's left to me to finish, and there's only one thing that will give my poor Jeremiah peace."

"No, Gretta, no," I said, struggling to rise, trying to grab the package from her hand. I fell back all but senseless, still gripped by the paralysis of the electric shock. I watched as if in a dream as Gretta moved about the kitchen, heating water on the stove, calmly making herself a cup of tea, and heaping into it a spoon of strychnine as though it were sugar.

Standing beside her the whole while was the young soldier. She talked to him in loving terms, and addressed me from time to time as well. She thanked me for a lovely Christmas Eve while I strove uselessly to break the paralysis, tears streaming from my eyes.

Then Gretta and her soldier left the kitchen. I heard her footsteps, inexplicably spritely, echoing down the hall. Her bedroom door shut.

And that, Jane, is the gist of a sad adventure. It was over. Oh, I had to suffer interviews with police and coroner. But it didn't take long, because, unfortunately, suicide is the commonest thing among the elderly. I was not pressed to tell the whole story, which they certainly would not have believed. As for myself, I suffered no ill aftereffects of the spiritual electrocution, which was, after all, less dangerous than actual electricity. In fact, if you will believe it, the next day I felt partially rejuvenated, and seem since that night to have gotten over my mild arthritis.

And now you may open the gift box I sent along, which said on it not to open until after you read my letter. As you will see, it is Gretta's paper fan. I bought it at the estate sale, together with a few other small mementos of a brief friendship.

You will observe that the fan, for all its simplicity, is of the finest craftsmanship, completely handmade in a manner not used in over half a century. When I first saw it, it was faded, dusty, and tattered to thinness as though occasionally sampled by moths. And the fan I've sent you *is* the same one, miraculously restored, as though cut and pasted recently, the classic floral design as bright as though painted yesterday.

I take this surprising restoration as evidence that Gretta is forgiven by Jeremiah and that they are now happily reunited—out there in the "somewhere" we're all destined one day and eternally to know.

Yours,
Penelope

# NOTES

## THE MYSTERIOUS DOOM OF JOSHUA WINFIELD

This story is considerably elaborated and retold from the traditional tale recorded by William Arnold in an article for the *Seattle Post-Intelligencer*, October 31, 1979, and reprinted in Carol J. Lind's self-published *Western Gothic* (1983).

## THE BARNACLE MAID

In 1938, Indian artist Charlie Edwards directed the carving of the Swinomish Reservation story pole. This story pole is a 61-foot cedar log with totem beasts and historical individuals depicted thereon: toads, bears, orcas, spirits, and even a representation of Franklin D. Roosevelt, who signed the bill that recognized the Samish people's right to self-government.

Preserved on this story pole is the tradition of a gigantic ghostly apparition in Deception Pass near the mouth of the Skagit River. In the 1960s, a Pierce County newspaperman, Emerson N. Matson, heard this story from Chief Martin Sampson himself. Chief Sampson rendered many great services for his tribe—and for the larger community of Washingtonians as well, lecturing at the University of Washington on Indian languages. I have retold Chief Sampson's tale from Matson's version, "The Maiden of Deception Pass," which appeared in *Longhouse Legends* (New York: Thomas Nelson, 1963).

## THE HAG'S HEAD OF ANGEL STREET

Except for the whimsically horrific climax, this story is entirely true and took place in a house on the actual Angel Street. The tale was told to me by Seattle horror author W. H. Pugmire, whom many will remember for his once-famed local rock fanzine *Punk Lust*, or for his earlier vampire shtick, performed in his youth at the greatly lamented Jones Fantastic Museum in the Seattle Center.

Of the event I've retold, Wilum adds, "My sister remembers more than I. I find it interesting that directly after this experience, I developed my deep love for horror films, which directly led to my maturing into an author of supernatural fiction."

## THE PHANTOM HOUND OF CHRISTMAS

The inspiration for this tale can be found in a column by Jean Godden, "Brutus the Dog's Sad End Is Turning into a Ghostly Tail," in the *Seattle Post-Intelligencer*, July 22, 1986. Poetic license has been taken in recreating experiences from the point of view of Brutus, but the ghostly parts of this retelling adhere one hundred percent to the facts.

## THE HEADLESS COLONEL

This ghost story adheres to the traditional accounts, known to many Coupeville residents of Whidbey Island. One published report is that of Kathryn Robinson in the *Seattle Weekly*, November 3, 1987. The epitaph that Penelope recites is from my wee poetry collection, *The Ghost Garden* (Liverpool, England: Dark Dreams Press, 1989).

## THE POOL OF THE MAPLE GOD

This story is retold from an account in D. W. Higgins's *The Mystic Spring and Other Tales of Western Life* (Toronto: William Briggs, 1904). It follows the actual events fairly closely, except that the present version combines two women into one. Annie, the first woman to see the pool demon, escaped and married her beau. Higgins reported that she, her children, and her grandchildren were all living in Victoria at the turn of the century. The second girl, who killed herself in the pool, was actually Julie Booth. I have streamlined the story, more by leaving certain things out than by inventing new additions.

## THE LAST PASSENGER

This tale is based on reports from the *News Review Umpqua Edition* of Roseburg, Oregon, for February 1973, and reprinted in *Western Gothic*. Lovola J. Bakken, of the Douglas County Museum, interviewed the people who occupied the Galesville farmhouse in the seventies and reported them to be serious and credible. They had experienced the appearance of the stagecoach at eleven o'clock every morning. Other phenomena were associated with the farmhouse as well, such as a *square* wine bottle leaping out of a wastebasket and skittering across the floor under its own power.

## THE FABULOUS SEA BELOW

Northwest Indian legends speak often of demonic underground

races. A typical example is reported by Ella E. Clark in her collection *Indian Legends of the Pacific Northwest* (Berkeley and Los Angeles: University of California Press, 1953). The tale regards a demon who lived in the secret passages under Vashon Island. An Indian youth's battle with this demon caused a great lake on Vashon to be sucked underground, which explains why Vashon has so little water today. Another legend has it that the very same Vashon tunnel comes out in Angle Lake in south King County. Up and down the coasts of Oregon, Washington, and British Columbia are legends of these subterranean passages. My modernized variation, set on Vancouver Island, was previously collected in a book of my short stories, *John Collier and Fredric Brown Went Quarrelling Through My Head* (Buffalo, New York: W. Paul Ganley, Publisher, 1989).

The hermit of this tale, Sam Keplemann, and his woodland hut are derived from a real person, who lived in just this manner near Des Moines in the late 1950s and early 1960s. Many improbable legends, designed to explain his odd life, arose among the children who harassed him.

## SERENE OMEN OF DEATH IN THE PIKE PLACE MARKET

Among the reports of this Market ghost are articles by columnist Rick Anderson that appeared in *The Seattle Times*: "Tall Tales and Rumor Put Some Spirit in the Pike Place Market," July 12, 1983; "If the Spirit Moves You, Check Out Old Haunts at Pike Place Market," October 31, 1984; "Ghost Stories: Early Enough to Get Scared," October 26, 1986; and "It's Time to Conjure Up Tales of Ghosts and Goblins," October 29, 1990. Many other reporters have written of this ghost as well. Additional elements are added from my own discussions with people when I worked in the Market. The whole is fictionalized, but may be compared with Anderson's reports for the traditional elements.

## THE FOREST IN THE LAKE

Various legends of sea monsters have been written about in Ella E. Clark's *Indian Legends of the Pacific Northwest* (Berkeley and Los Angeles: University of California Press, 1953); Clarence B. Bagley's *Indian Myths of the Northwest* (Seattle: Lowman & Hanford,

1930); "Luhr Lore" in the newsletter of the Nisqually Nature Center (Summer 1990); "Nisqually Mythology" in the *Overland Monthly*, volume 32, 1898; David M. Buerge's "Sacred Burien" in the *Seattle Weekly*, January 1989; and many such places.

The "octopus tale" in the early part is entirely true and did not need embellishment. The second half is just as obviously fabulous, but only in its treatment of the octopuslike monster. The underwater forest itself is attested to by Northwest divers. My father and uncle, who were professional divers in the 1970s, explored the underwater forest. I have taken the descriptions from them.

## THE OVAL DRAGON

This Victorian fishermen's legend of the Point Defiance sea monster was reprinted on August 14, 1970, in Tacoma's *Morning News Tribune*, and found its way from there into Carol J. Lind's charming self-published book, *Western Gothic*. Sea serpent legends, and especially legends about lake serpents, are encountered throughout the Northwest, but the description of the oval serpent is unique. Whether one is inclined to believe in monsters of the sea or not,

the story has nonetheless proved its sturdiness as a doozy of a Northwest traditional tale.

## LEGEND OF THE WHITE EAGLE SALOON

The conversations in this story are invented reconstructions from my own imagination and do not represent the people for whom they are named. The main incidents, however, are vouchsafed by the real witnesses Chuck Hughes and Anne Audry. Their story came to me in the form of an otherwise undated clipping from a May 1992 issue of *The Oregonian*. The article is called "Shots in the Dark," by Kristian Foden-Vencil. Penelope's experiences in the upstairs room are added.

## SARAH, THE GHOST OF GEORGETOWN CASTLE

Reporter Rick Anderson has written that as many as three dozen people claimed to have seen the Georgetown Castle ghost, but his was a low estimate. She has been the subject of an afternoon television program; I've heard people discuss her on local radio talk shows; and Paul Andrews wrote at length in *Pacific Magazine* about the surprising experiences of Ray McWade and

Petter Petterson while they were living in the castle. Ray and Petter have been fictionalized as Jay and Pat, but the incidents per se are authentic and unchanged.

## FRITZ, THE GENTLE GHOST OF SHAW ISLAND

The tale of Fritz is derived from Don Towksbury's article, "Ghost House? Not Seeing Is Believing" in the *Seattle Post-Intelligencer*, January 19, 1987; my retelling conforms exactly to the facts given in this case, without elaboration. As an aside, Jane Bradshaw's story of "Joan" (by British writer Mary Ann Allen) can be found in my Tor Books anthology *Tales by Moonlight, Volume I.*

## OGOPOGO

Among the innumerable sources for Ogopogo are these: "Kelowna" by E. Jervis Bloomfield in *The Seattle Times*, November 18, 1962; "Lake Okanagan Still Hides Slimy Ogopogo" in the *Daily Olympian* for July 25, 1977; "Okanagan's Loch Ness Monster" by Joel Connelly in the *Seattle Post-Intelligencer*, July 24, 1977; and "The Elusive Ogopogo" in Carol J. Lind's *Western Gothic* (1983).

## THE QUEEN MUM

Mrs. Mary Woods purportedly died a few months shy of 121 years of age. But one does wonder. I learned of her from an undated KXAS radio script, delivered on the air in the 1950s by Northwest novelist and historian Nard Jones, and preserved by Pacific National Bank in a series of the published scripts called *Northwest Narratives*. As for Anna-Chrissy—after reading her letter to Penelope, I rather worry about her state of health.

## JEREMIAH

This most frightening of the Penelope Pettiweather stories is entirely my invention, except that the scariest part, Alzheimer's syndrome, is all too real. The story was published originally in a limited edition pamphlet along with two other of Penelope's adventures, in *Harmless Ghosts* (Runcorn, England: The Haunted Library, 1990), which was instantly out of print. This is the tale's first U.S. publication. The Jane Bradshaw story alluded to in this story, "The Gravedigger and Death," can be found in my Tor Books anthology *Tales by Moonlight, Volume II.*

*Dear Reader,*

*The tales of Penelope Pettiweather, ghost detector, are fiction, and I, of course, am not Penelope. But a lot of her is in me, and I certainly share her fascination with the supernatural. I am very interested in receiving tales of ghosts encountered throughout the Pacific Northwest. I invite your letters from Oregon, Washington, Idaho, Montana, and British Columbia, regarding localized traditions, personal experiences, or family legends of ghosts and strange beasties. If a second volume of tales results, I will protect the identities of those who do not wish to be cited by name, while crediting the sources for those who do wish credit. Please write me in care of Sasquatch Books, 1931 Second Avenue, Seattle, Washington 98101. And by the way—thanks for buying my humble book.*

*Thine,*
*Jessica*

## ABOUT THE AUTHOR

JESSICA AMANDA SALMONSON is a recipient of the World Fantasy Award and the Lambda Award. Her books include *What Did Miss Darrington See?: Feminist Supernatural Stories of the 19th and 20th Century* from the Feminist Press; *Tales by Moonlight* from Tor Books; *The Encyclopedia of Amazons* from Paragon House and Doubleday; and a horror novel, *Anthony Shriek*, set in the streets of Seattle, from Dell Abyss Books. Her short stories have appeared in numerous anthologies in five languages. She is presently at work on a book of feminist mysticism. Ms. Salmonson lives in Seattle.